Collaborative Advantage

"A must-read for every innovator and transformator!"
—Franziska Tschudi Sauber, *President of the Board, Weidmann Group*

"Not heroic foresight but focus on own strengths and open collaboration is what enables successful transformation – an inspirational and practical guide for how to get it done."
—Christoph Loos, *Chairman of the Board of Directors, Hilti Group*

"*Collaborative Advantage* is packed with great examples and useful insights into innovating for the future. It is an essential guide for anyone interested in Open Innovation."
—Henry Chesbrough, *Author of Open Innovation, Professor at Luiss University in Rome, and the Haas School of Business at UC Berkeley*

"In today's dynamic markets, companies need to collaborate to have access to all assets and capabilities necessary to out-innovate competitors. However, to collaborate effectively is an organizational capability that needs to be build and nurtured. This book shows how."
—Claudio Feser, *Senior Partner Emeritus & Co-Founder Leadership Practice McKinsey & Company*

"*Collaborative Advantage* is the overarching framework in which different elements like business model innovation, modern creative methods and management adaptation to the VUCA-world are combined to build a playbook which can directly be used by management to implement the necessary transformations to survive in a uncertain and unstable future world.

The book is founded on sound scientific research. Nonetheless it offers a practical and easy access to implementation.

A very recommended book for all who want their company excel in the next years."
—Luigi Pedrocchi, *Group CEO Mibelle Group (2000–2022)*

"This book delves into the essence of business transformation, I felt it provides valuable insights into unique styles of leadership that foster innovation and collaboration, leading to favorable outcomes."
—Roshni Nadar, *Chairperson HCL Technologies, Forbes "The worlds 100 most powerful women"*

"Transformation is a necessity in the new business environment. Collaborative Advantage outlines how to do it in a sustainable way."

—Marianne Janik, *CEO Microsoft Germany*

"If you're a transformational leader in an aging industry seeking innovation and growth, look no further. Oliver & Raphael's captivating & very practical insights on growth through collaborations and partnerships is the beacon you've been searching for."

—Rashmi Kasat, *VP Digital Technologies, Metso*

"If you and your company want to be successful in tomorrow's world – Collaborative Advantage is a must read! In a Hyper-VUCA world, adaptability, entrepreneurship, speed and leveraged ecosystems are key for a successful transformation."

—Stephan Seifert, *CEO Körber Group*

"In a world where competitiveness is no longer enough, Collaborative Advantage provides a groundbreaking framework for achieving success through collaboration, innovation, and transformation!"

—Dr. Stephanie Schoss, *Founder C Talks*

Raphael Bömelburg · Oliver Gassmann

Collaborative Advantage

How Open Organizations Thrive in Volatility

Raphael Bömelburg
University of St. Gallen
St. Gallen, Switzerland

Oliver Gassmann
University of St. Gallen
St. Gallen, Switzerland

ISBN 978-3-031-36305-4   ISBN 978-3-031-36306-1   (eBook)
https://doi.org/10.1007/978-3-031-36306-1

© The Editor(s) (if applicable) and The Author(s), under exclusive license to Springer Nature Switzerland AG 2024

This work is subject to copyright. All rights are solely and exclusively licensed by the Publisher, whether the whole or part of the material is concerned, specifically the rights of reprinting, reuse of illustrations, recitation, broadcasting, reproduction on microfilms or in any other physical way, and transmission or information storage and retrieval, electronic adaptation, computer software, or by similar or dissimilar methodology now known or hereafter developed.
The use of general descriptive names, registered names, trademarks, service marks, etc. in this publication does not imply, even in the absence of a specific statement, that such names are exempt from the relevant protective laws and regulations and therefore free for general use.
The publisher, the authors, and the editors are safe to assume that the advice and information in this book are believed to be true and accurate at the date of publication. Neither the publisher nor the authors or the editors give a warranty, expressed or implied, with respect to the material contained herein or for any errors or omissions that may have been made. The publisher remains neutral with regard to jurisdictional claims in published maps and institutional affiliations.

This Palgrave Macmillan imprint is published by the registered company Springer Nature Switzerland AG
The registered company address is: Gewerbestrasse 11, 6330 Cham, Switzerland

Acknowledgements

This book would not be possible but for the willingness of remarkable leaders to share their personal learnings and reflections with us. We would like to thank in particular Jose Manuel Barroso (European Commission), Alexander Birken (Otto), Yves Daccord (International Red Cross), Mathias Döpfner (Springer), John Hennessey (Alphabet/Google), Roshni Nadar (HCL Technologies), Satya Nadella (Microsoft), Marco Meyrat (Hilti), Carsten Koerl (Sportradar), and Ian Roberts (Bühler) for providing us with their invaluable insights. We further thank Nicole Marxer, Johanna Knapp, and Michelle Janssen for their instrumental support in preparing this book.

Contents

Part I Collaborative Advantage

1 Introduction: Managing in a Hyper-VUCA World — 3
- 1.1 From Predicting the Future to Creating the Future — 5
- 1.2 A New Kind of Advantage — 6
- 1.3 Toward High Performance in a Hyper-VUCA World — 8
- 1.4 How to Use the Book — 9

2 Collaboration Analytics — 11
- 2.1 Understanding the Signatures Within Your Company: It's All About the Patterns — 14
- 2.2 The Ideation Signature — 15
- 2.3 The Influence Signature — 15
- 2.4 The Efficiency Signature — 16
- 2.5 The Innovation Signature — 17
- 2.6 The Silo Signature — 18
- 2.7 The Vulnerability Signature — 18
- 2.8 The Agility Signature — 20
- 2.9 Culture Analytics Through Digital Footprints — 20
- 2.10 Toward a Data-Driven Future of Leadership? — 21
- 2.11 The Next Step — 23

Part II Collaborative Innovation

3 Dynamics of Collaborative Innovation — 29
- 3.1 Co-create Your Future Business with Customers — 29
- 3.2 Break Up Internal Echo Chambers to Drive Idea Flow — 33
- 3.3 Use Leadership Incentives to Nurture Innovation Across Silos — 36
- 3.4 Understand the Benefits of Social Learning — 40
- 3.5 Build a Culture of Creative Collisions — 41

4 Leading for Collaborative Innovation — 47
- 4.1 Lead for Collisions, Not for More Meetings — 47
- 4.2 Balance Internal and External Collaboration — 54
- 4.3 Connect Networks of Innovators — 57
- 4.4 Three Take-Aways for Leaders — 64
- 4.5 Ideas for Action: Simple Practices — 66
- 4.6 Ideas for Action: Advanced Practices — 67
- 4.7 Collaborative Innovation in Action: LEGO — 68
- 4.8 The Next Step — 70

Part III Collaborative Scaling

5 Hyperscaling Through Collaborations — 75
- 5.1 Leverage Your Ecosystem to Scale Up Faster — 75
- 5.2 Leverage Collaborative Networks to Scale Organically — 81
- 5.3 Scale Faster by Scaling Lean and Orchestrating External Partners — 87
- 5.4 Lead with a Focus on Collaboration to Energize Scaling — 91
- 5.5 Employ Nudges to Help Your Scale-Up Team Resonate — 95

6 Managing Growth Challenges Through Collaborative Scaling — 101
- 6.1 Increase Collaborations in a Targeted Manner — 101
- 6.2 Improve Quality of Collaborations — 106
- 6.3 Vulnerability as a Leader Helps You Nurture Resonance — 110
- 6.4 Leverage Failures to Grow Collaborations — 116
- 6.5 Balance Structure and Autonomy to Manage the Scaling Trap — 118
- 6.6 Three Take-Aways for Leaders — 121
- 6.7 Ideas for Action: Simple Practices — 122
- 6.8 Ideas for Action: Advanced Practices — 123

6.9	Collaborative Scaling in Action at Amazon	124
	6.9.1 Collaborative Analytics at Amazon	127
	6.9.2 Scaling Up Infrastructure on Demand/ Infrastructure as a Service	128
6.10	The Next Step	130

Part IV Collaborative Transformation

7 Overcoming Corporate Silos — 135

7.1	Disrupt Rigid Collaborations to Increase Openness to Change	135
7.2	Apply Leadership Rotations to Foster a Unified Vision	142
7.3	Use Collaborative Incentives to Energize Transformation	144
7.4	Build on Joint Field Trips to Align Departments Behind Transformation	147
7.5	Use Local Empowerment to Transform Your Organizations into a Leader-Leader System	151
7.6	Employ Collaborative Incentives to Drive Behavior Change More Effectively	154
7.7	Spark a Movement Behind Your Transformation by Connecting Change-Agents	161
7.8	Assemble a Diverse Coalition to Increase Adaptability	166
7.9	Combine Internal and External Collaborative Structures	170

8 Leveraging Partnerships for Transformation — 179

8.1	Apply Collaborative Practices to Maintain Your Advantage as You Grow	179
8.2	Bring Collaborative Practices to New Organizations	182
8.3	Combine Autonomy and Synergy to Leverage the Transformation Potential of Acquisitions	184
8.4	Three Take-Aways for Managers	189
8.5	Ideas for Action: Simple Practices	190
8.6	Ideas for Action: Advanced Practices	190
8.7	Collaborative Transformation in Action: Microsoft	191
8.8	The Next Step	195

Index 197

About the Authors

Raphael Bömelburg combines a Ph.D. in Management with a Master's degree in Psychology and international work experience in the technology sector. Building on this multidisciplinary background, he is interested in emerging business opportunities in the intersection of Psychology and Technology. He advises multinational companies on data-driven transformation and technology-enabled business models. Raphael conducted research at institutions such as Stanford University, the University of Miami, the Excellence Cluster Languages of Emotions, and the Rotterdam School of Management. He is currently a lecturer and fellow at the University of St. Gallen.

Stay up to date and connect at: https://www.linkedin.com/in/raphael-boemelburg/.

Oliver Gassmann is Full Professor of Technology and Innovation Management at the University of St. Gallen, Switzerland. After completing his Ph.D. in 1996, he was leading Corporate Research at Schindler Corporation. Gassmann has been recognized as one of the most active innovation scholars (IAMOT), and as one of the leading economists of Germany (FAZ). In 2014 he was awarded the Scholarly Impact Award by the Journal of Management, in 2015 the Citation of Excellence Award by the Emerald Group. Gassmann has founded several spin-off companies and serves in boards of international companies and institutions.

List of Figures

Fig. 1.1	The high-performance cycle in a hyper-VUCA world	8
Fig. 2.1	Cross-departmental collaborations	12
Fig. 2.2	Team-level view of cross-departmental collaborations	13
Fig. 2.3	Collaboration signature of ideation	16
Fig. 2.4	Collaboration signature of influence	16
Fig. 2.5	Collaboration signature of efficiency	17
Fig. 2.6	Collaboration signature of innovation	18
Fig. 2.7	Collaboration signature of silos	19
Fig. 2.8	Collaboration signature of vulnerability	19
Fig. 2.9	Collaboration signature of agility	20
Fig. 2.10	Data-driven management of intangible resources	24
Fig. 5.1	Idea-execution link	81
Fig. 6.1	Global Expert Network at Halliburton, stylized for clarity and simplicity	103
Fig. 6.2	Global Expert Network at Halliburton after changes, stylized for clarity and simplicity	105
Fig. 6.3	Team of Teams at TLGG Consulting	120
Fig. 7.1	Incentive scheme of the red balloon challenge	161
Fig. 7.2	Combination of formal hierarchy and flexible, boundary-spanning instant organization driven by personal relations	167

Part I

Collaborative Advantage

1

Introduction: Managing in a Hyper-VUCA World

> *The pessimist complains about the wind.*
> *The optimist expects it to change.*
> *The leader adjusts the sails.*
> —John Maxwell

Your job as a manager has never been harder. The world is changing at an unprecedented pace, and yesterday's success recipes quickly can become the baggage slowing you down while established competitors or new entrants race ahead. The seemingly constant influx of external shocks and technological disruption challenge organizations even as shareholders demand returns and employees rising salaries and job security. Consider the events to which executives had to respond to from 2020 to 2023 alone:

- *Technological disruption*: A steady stream of potentially revolutionary innovations has forced managers to continually assess and reassess their own business. The speed of development has accelerated: In 2021, our assessment of the opportunities for innovation created by AI for innovation drew huge attention, becoming one of the year's most cited articles; less than a year later, the reality of ChatGPT surpassed all forecasts of what generative AI would be able to do when. Quantum computing is arriving

---

Volatile, uncertain, complex and ambiguous

© The Author(s), under exclusive license to Springer Nature Switzerland AG 2024
R. Bömelburg and O. Gassmann, *Collaborative Advantage*,
https://doi.org/10.1007/978-3-031-36306-1_1

rapidly. Augmented and virtual reality are enabled in web 3.0 environments, with non-fungible tokens (NFTs) as the first strong use cases. In drug discovery, companies like the US start-up Insilico are revolutionizing the innovation process by combining AI analytics with drug design [1]. And most companies have their hands full just adapting to more mature technologies, nevermind AI: Migrating your infrastructure into the cloud, while optimizing production through IoT, setting up e-commerce platforms and switching from direct mails to integrated omni-channel marketing is…well, a tall order [2].

- *Geopolitical risks*: Russian aggression in Ukraine and Western sanctions in response sent shocks into energy and many commodity markets. In Asia, tensions flared over the autonomy of Taiwan, a country that produces more than half of the world's semi-conductors [3]. The increasing rivalry between the United States and China has reversed a long-running trend for global integration: Foreign direct investment between the US and China dropped by 96 percent between 2016 and 2020 [6]. The question of who controls technologies that are perceived as strategically relevant, such as 5G, is becoming more contentious. As tech-ecosystems increasingly decouple along the lines of political spheres of influence, organizations have to choose where to place their bets.
- *Supply chain shocks*: These geopolitical tensions have exacerbated the effect of Covid-related lockdowns, which were already exposing the vulnerability of supply chains. After decades of cost-optimization in logistics and manufacturing, near-shoring and diversification are back in fashion in order to build up resilience: In 2021, two-thirds of multinational corporations said they were considering changes to their supply chains [4].
- *Inflation and the risk of stagflation*: Supply chain shocks coupled with stimulus money have caused a surge of inflation which is projected to remain above target for the foreseeable future. Price-stability is in flux, and sluggish growth raises the specter of stagflation [5]. Tightening monetary policy in response to inflation pressures has pushed managers into unfamiliar territory: up to now, many have operated almost exclusively in environments with abundant cheap capital.
- *Climate change*: Companies are under enormous pressure from a range of stakeholders to reduce their carbon footprints. As public concern mounts in response to extreme weather events, consumer trends are shifting. This has opened up new opportunities in areas such as electric vehicles, energy storage, and battery recycling, but also challenged other industries. Reporting is an added challenge: publicly listed companies are increasingly

expected to provide sophisticated assessments of their exposure to climate risk [7].
- *Political fragmentation*: Political polarization and identity politics have meant younger customers and employees in particular are making new demands on companies: Do you share my values? How do you advance the causes which I care about? Up to 90 percent of Gen Z and Millennial customers strive to support brands whose purposes align with their values, according to one assessment [8].
- *Black Swan events*: Managers have always known their companies need to be ready for sudden and unknowable events, but the Black Swan poster child, the COVID pandemic, made this knowledge palpable.

Confronted with a world that is extremely volatile, uncertain, complex, and ambiguous [hyper-VUCA], many managers chase these external changes—racing after market trends in the latest industry reports, conducting risk assessments, and discussing in boardrooms the game-changing potential of emerging technologies. The problem with this approach is that there are always more new trends and potentially disruptive changes to consider, leading to paralysis by analysis. On the other end of the extreme, companies can break out into a flurry of activities in the name of strategic "agility." This is how organizations end up with 14 top priorities and a myriad of constantly changing strategic initiatives. This activity without a consistent focus, and operating in constant emergency mode, burns out organizations without leading to superior performance.

1.1 From Predicting the Future to Creating the Future

A man who wants to lead the orchestra must turn his back on the crowd.—James Crook

The best entrepreneurs—people who thrive in hyper-VUCA environments—are deeply skeptical of these attempts at strategic foresight. Instead of chasing after external trends and trying to predict scenarios, they shift the focus to their own strengths and capabilities. They see that the answer to where to steer your company is already there. But it is not in analyses of external trends. Instead, it is in your own employees, your customers, and the partners in your ecosystem. Through these crucial resources, you can shape the future instead of chasing after it. After all, the best way to predict the future is to create it.

This shift in thinking changes the game. Organizations that try to race behind external trends tend to feel like they are on a roller coaster: The high speed is being imposed on them; they are not in control. Organizations that focus on their own strengths to create the future feel like they're at the wheel of a sports car: the speed can still be dizzying, but they are in control. How to step off the roller coaster and into the driver's seat? By doing it together.

1.2 A New Kind of Advantage

Steve Jobs might seem like our counterexample, the ultimate exemplar of bending "heroic foresight" into managerial success. Apple's renewal in the 2000s started with the iPod, a product which set the company on the incredible journey from a struggling computer manufacturer to becoming the world's most valuable public company. Let's take a look at how this success was achieved.

- The idea: The iPod actually started with one of Apple's partners. Tony Fadell, an engineer working for Philips, approached Apple with his idea for an MP3 player complemented by an online music store. Apple hired him as an independent contractor to pursue the idea.
- The product: Recognizing the huge potential in Fadell's idea, Apple assembled a team of 35 people from partner companies such as Philips, Ideo, General Magic, Connectix, and WebTV. Apple was unwilling to take resources away from its core Mac line, but by leveraging this partner-talent, the company was nonetheless able to develop the iPod with incredible speed: The first generation of the device was shipped just ten months after its initial conception.
- The technology stack: You could argue the true genius of the iPod was the platform business model, which Apple later replicated with the App Store. But neither was this Steve Job's, or even another Apple employee's idea. Apple had to pay a license fee of 15 dollars per iPod to a consortium of Wolfson, Toshiba, and Texas Instruments for the portal player technology, the core of iTunes.

Steve Jobs didn't manage the successful turnaround of Apple on his own. Instead, Apple consistently built its success on an ability to orchestrate ideas, resources, and technology from customers, employees, and partners. While the story of the visionary designer is appealing, a look behind the curtain reveals less the iGod of Jobs and more the weGod of Apple's ecosystem as the driving force behind Apple's renaissance. The technology that the "outsider" Fadell helped create is today responsible for over half of global revenues at Apple. In case you are now worried about Fadell's cut of the pie, we can assure you he's doing just fine: He went on to found Nest labs, which was acquired by Google, making him a billionaire. In 2014, *Time Magazine* nominated him as one of the most influential people on earth.

This collaborative approach is not unique to Apple. Companies from Daimler to 3M, Google, and IBM have built some of their most iconic success stories on the systematic use of alliances, networks, and ecosystems.

Louis Gerstner reinvented IBM through a crowdsourcing effort to which over 300,000 employees contributed. Satya Nadella managed one the most remarkable transformations of the twenty-first century by turning Microsoft from a monopolist to an open, collaborative company orchestrating partner resources throughout its ecosystem. Manufacturers such as Procter & Gamble replaced their traditional research and development teams with a collaborative "connect and develop" department. Cisco out-innovated the much more prestigious and better-resourced Bell Labs through an open approach based on collaborations and acquisitions.

This new approach goes beyond the traditional idea of competitive advantage. For decades, managers were taught based on Michael Porter's classic framework: Competitive advantage was the result of superior positioning in the competitive landscape. By analyzing and predicting the external world, managers could find the optimal niche where their company could capture outsized value.

The problem with this approach in a hyper-VUCA world, of course, is that the world changes too quickly and too unpredictably: No positioning in the external world is a sustainable source of competitive advantage. Instead, exceptional leaders and organizations are increasingly stepping off of Porter's prescribed path. Instead of analyzing their competition, they focus on their own capabilities. Instead of predicting the future, they create it. Instead of building barriers to entry, they build an open ecosystem by leveraging resources around them. Instead of winning through competitive advantage, they win through the adaptability and speed they achieve through *collaborative advantage*.

What do we mean by collaborative advantage? For the purposes of this book, we loosely define it as the capability of an organization to leverage resources inside and outside of its formal boundaries to create and capture value. In today's world, openness and connectivity are the keys to success.

Ecosystems and open networks are the source of competitive advantage. Collaborative advantage is achieved when companies focus on their strengths and partner together in order to create superior, innovative value propositions for their customers and dominate new, uncontested market spaces. These companies create win-win-win situations for their customers, their partners, their employees, and, in the end, their shareholders. They innovate by making the world their lab instead of making the lab their world.

So what is required for creating the future?

1.3 Toward High Performance in a Hyper-VUCA World

Successful companies create the future by constantly cycling through three steps: First, they co-create new and superior offerings (*Innovate*). This requires the sensing of new opportunities, successful experimentation alongside assessing customer needs, and discipline in killing off marginal successes in order to focus all their energy on potential rocket ships. Second, they take innovations which have product-market fit and make them dominant in that market (*Scale*). This requires a switch from building products to building systems and partnerships, as well as managing the escalating complexity that comes with hypergrowth. Finally, before the new solution becomes irrelevant, they renew their capabilities in order to successfully co-develop the next generation of offerings (*Transform*). This requires challenging dominant logic, empowering new leaders, and experimenting with new ways of working.

High performance in a hyper-VUCA world (Fig. 1.1).

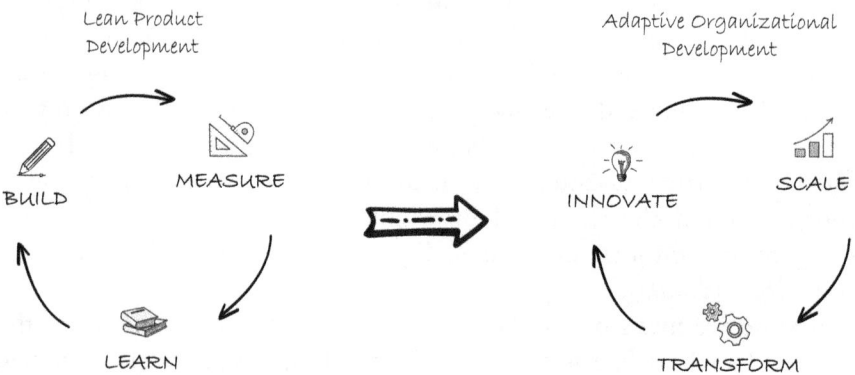

Fig. 1.1 The high-performance cycle in a hyper-VUCA world

Consider how this cycle explains the success of Amazon. The company started by innovating, and developed an e-commerce solution through which it initially sold books. After achieving initial product-market fit, the company-built systems and leveraged their ecosystem to scale up the e-commerce platform. By enabling marketplace transactions and opening up their product to external sellers, they turbocharged growth. Finally, they proactively transformed and refocused their capabilities in cloud computing for enterprise customers. Through this cycle, Amazon has increased annual revenues from 34 billion dollars in 2010 to 470 billion in 2021—and Amazon Web Services, the company's cloud offering, and the innovations related to it are leading growth going forward.

Product development has been revolutionized in recent years: The classical stage-gate process has been replaced with the lean build-measure-learn cycle. We propose a similar change for organizations. Replace long-term strategies with an adaptive cycle: *Innovate-Scale-Transform.*

1.4 How to Use the Book

The goal of this book is to provide you with actionable, tangible guidance as you build on collaborative advantage and co-create the future for your own organization. In the next chapter, we will focus on understanding how collaborative your organization already is and how efficiently you leverage external resources. How do innovative ideas from outside your organization flow into and through your organization? How flexibly does your organization scale promising new ventures through leveraging and recombining resources throughout your ecosystem? And where in your organization are rigid islands of resistance that inhibit the transformation and development of new capabilities? Increasingly, all of these questions can be answered in real time, based on minimally intrusive digital footprints of employees. As your organization competes in a networked world, you will need to make informed decisions about how to orchestrate these networks.

Parts II, III, and IV provide deep dives into the three steps of the adaptive cycle: Innovate, Scale, and Transform. Each of the parts brims with practical examples, cutting edge research, and leadership insights that help show how you can unleash the power of collaborations to co-create the future. All of them feature a diverse set of ideas for action which range from simple, hands-on changes you can implement next Monday to more transformative ideas that might take longer—but which will move your organization to the next level. As you read, you will develop a tangible and action-oriented understanding of how collaborative advantage works in practice. In our experience coaching executives, this understanding is a great basis for reflecting on your own organization's potential for collaborative advantage.

To help you get to important and actionable insights as quickly as possible, we have included "Lessons Learned" sections in all chapters, which summarize key take-aways, as well as "Self-reflections" inviting you to transfer insights into your own work environment and "Quick wins," which offer concrete ideas for turning the ideas in the book into actions that benefit your organization.

In order to make this book as valuable and useful for you as possible, we have spoken with the leaders behind some of the most successful and innovative organizations on the planet. John Henessey, chairman of Alphabet, talked to us about using external partnerships to position Google for the future. Satya Nadella, chief executive of Microsoft, highlighted how he shifted the software giant's culture toward openness. Roshni Nadar, chairwoman of HCL Technologies and one the most powerful businesswomen of Asia, explained to us the crucial balance between organic, internally driven, and rewarded innovation and an aggressive acquisition and partner strategy. Yves Daccord, former director general of the international red cross, impressed upon us the importance of real-time collaboration and leadership when lives are on the line. Throughout our research and interviews with leaders such as these, a central theme emerged:

> If your organization stops to grow as a business, you have to start to grow as a leader. Let's take the first steps together!

References

In order to keep the book lean enough to comfortably be read on a plane, we have listed the full references on the companion website for your convenience. If you want to dig deeper, please check them out here:

1. Collaborative-advantage.org/references-introduction/1.
2. Collaborative-advantage.org/references-introduction/2.
3. Collaborative-advantage.org/references-introduction/3.
4. Collaborative-advantage.org/references-introduction/4.
5. Collaborative-advantage.org/references-introduction/5.
6. Collaborative-advantage.org/references-introduction/6.
7. Collaborative-advantage.org/references-introduction/7.
8. Collaborative-advantage.org/references-introduction/8.

2

Collaboration Analytics

> *What gets measured gets managed.*
> —Peter Drucker

As a leader, you need to know how your organization works. You think you know? Certainly, how your organization *really* works has nothing to do with handbooks, prescribed processes, or organizational charts. Your picture is much clearer once you see how your employees work together and interact with one another, how they team up to achieve common goals, how they communicate formally and informally. In a small team, this might be easy to assess, as you might be part of the interaction. But the larger the team gets and the more the company is connected with the outside world, the more unreliable your intuition becomes.

Transforming your business means dealing with uncertainty: Are you pursuing the right goals? Is what you are doing working? Are you building capabilities that will make your organization successful in the coming years? Making judgment calls on whether you are going in the right direction and moving at the right speed is incredibly hard. It might, however, be getting easier.

Increasingly, advances in analytical tools and data availability allow us to conduct in-depth, unobtrusive, and real-time assessments of the collaborative soft factors in an organization—patterns of collaboration that we term collaboration signatures: By understanding patterns of advice-seeking, you can reveal hidden influencers and boost their impact. By identifying silos and

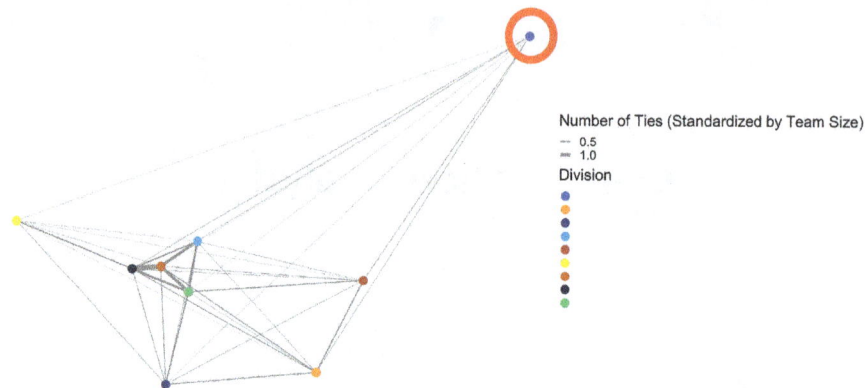

Fig. 2.1 Cross-departmental collaborations

removing bottlenecks, you can boost the flow of ideas and resources. Adding a navigation system to a plane makes it so much easier for the pilot to control where it goes. Similarly, an objective assessment of the culture and collaboration in your organization will allow you to manage your transformation with confidence because you can understand the impact of your transformation initiatives in real time. By making soft factors measurable, you make them manageable.

For example, let's say you are reorganizing your organization to support business model innovations that require multiple departments to collaborate in new ways. Wouldn't it be nice to have a dashboard that lets you see how these collaborations are developing? (Fig. 2.1).

This was the case for a fast-moving consumer goods company in Central Europe with which we worked. The company's business model, wherein its products were sold at supermarkets, was under pressure. High labor costs and increased competition from cheaper competitors were making it difficult to remain profitable. As such, the company's management was on the lookout for alternative sources of revenue, including experimenting with offering subscriptions to consumers through e-commerce channels. This sent new challenges cascading down the hierarchy: Employees in marketing had to learn about online marketing, logistics teams had to learn to deal with smaller batches and faster changes in production lines, and product developers had to learn to innovate for end customers rather than retailers. To facilitate this innovation, the company embarked on a transformation initiative with a reorganization toward cross-functional collaboration as its centerpiece.

Throughout the transformation process, we collected real-time data on collaboration by tracking the digital interactions between employees from different departments. We enriched this data with pulse-check surveys on

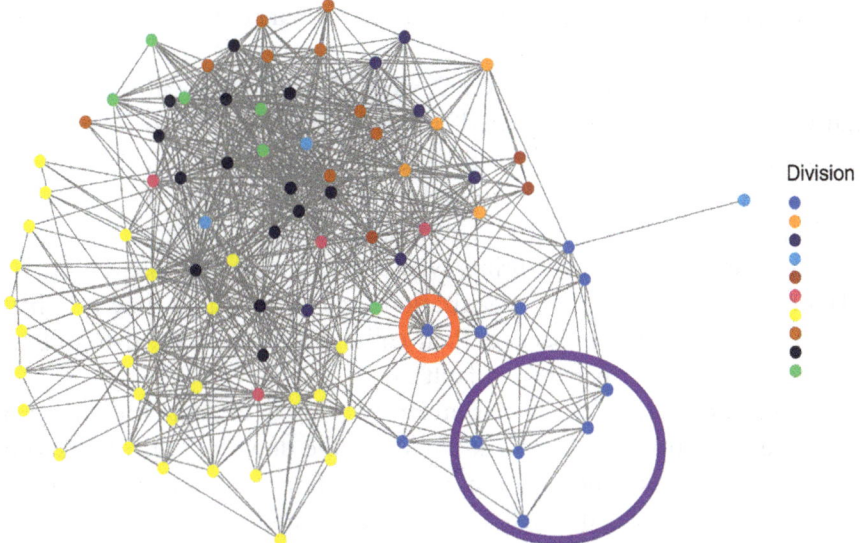

Fig. 2.2 Team-level view of cross-departmental collaborations

innovation, leadership, and performance. A first dashboard at the department level (pictured above) identified a core-periphery structure, with some departments collaborating closely together (the beating heart of the organization) and others remaining on the periphery. One department, however, was a complete outlier in operating almost wholly separately from the rest of the organization.

Zooming in revealed that this isolation was a function of interactions at the team level. When cross-departmental collaboration worked, it was because it was facilitated through a single "broker team" in the isolated department. The majority of other teams in this department had no cross-departmental collaborations at all (Fig. 2.2).

This identified the broker team as a bottleneck for the flow of ideas throughout the organization and highlighted the potential to increase and diversify collaboration by bringing in more peripheral teams and better distributing cross-departmental collaboration.

The company's management was also interested in the collaboration signatures associated with success in their context: What were the innovative units doing differently from those that were not proposing or developing changes to the business model? We identified a collaboration signature that was internally egalitarian and cohesive. At the same time, external collaboration was diverse, highly energetic, and focused. This signature was associated with increased performance across a variety of performance measures—by about 20 percent.

In addition to providing the CEO with a clear and detailed picture of what was happening "on the ground" in his organization, the assessment also reinforced an intervention: Through targeted sprints, cross-functional teams were selected to bridge departments and work on a set of previously identified high-impact challenges. The results of these sprints were presented to the full company. Members of these sprints were found to have almost double the collaborative reach across the organization, and at the same time also have had a highly energizing impact on their colleagues. In essence, they fulfilled bridging roles across departmental fault lines.

Through the analysis, the management was able to evaluate the impact of their reorganization in real time. It could double down on what worked in the connected core of the organization, and refine what wasn't working in the isolated department through a data-driven understanding of the mechanisms behind it, such as the overloaded bottleneck-team. By understanding which collaboration signatures were delivering the desired outcomes (cross-departmental business innovation), managers were able to design tailored sprints that turbocharged the transformation.

2.1 Understanding the Signatures Within Your Company: It's All About the Patterns

> In God we trust, all others bring data.—W. Edwards Deming

How can you develop such a data-driven understanding of the collaboration signatures in your organization? It is becoming easier and easier to unobtrusively assess the real culture rather than just the perceived one. Just as the Internet of Things (IoT) revolution has allowed us to analyze our customers' processes by enhancing physical products with sensors and linking them through cloud technology, the explosion of digital tools in the workplace enables us to measure how work and collaboration take place in our organizations.

Today, the average knowledge worker uses 35 business apps—a trend that is set to increase. In all of these apps, employees leave digital footprints that can be used to construct the "digital twins" of an organization's practices. Some of the easiest footprints to analyze are collaborative interactions.

A great way to get started with this kind of data is to plot the collaboration patterns in your dashboard, as we have shown in the introductory case. Research has consistently linked certain collaboration signatures to relevant strategic outcomes such as innovation, efficiency, and agility. By spotting these signatures in your organization, you can develop a hands-on, data-driven bird's eye view of how your employees collaborate—and which knock-on outcomes you can expect. You get a detailed map where what type of change would help you achieve your goals. Through plotting changes over time, you can understand the impact your transformation initiative is having on the ground in real time.

Fortunately, research has identified specific patterns which predict organizational performance [1].

2.2 The Ideation Signature

The ideation signature allows you to identify employees who are likely to produce creative ideas. Innovation is often perceived as a social process, but we tend to overvalue the number of interactions required for inspiration. In reality, the reach of our collaborations is much more important than the size of our network: While the focal employee on the left side of Fig. 2.3 collaborates regularly with only four other employees, each of these is largely independent of one another and thus provides fresh perspectives. In contrast, the focal employee on the right has six colleagues he works with regularly, but because they all belong to the same group, they will generally have similar opinions and make similar assumptions. They are likely to produce ideas that are likely to be fairly uniform and familiar.

The core of the ideation signature: Being connected to people who are not connected to each other.

2.3 The Influence Signature

The influence signature allows you to identify informal leaders and opinion shapers (Fig. 2.4). These individuals are important in any transformation that requires the buy-in of a critical mass of employees. While we often focus on formal leaders as multipliers for such efforts, employees also look to informal leaders and influencers when deciding whether to change their behavior. Importantly, research has shown that informal influencers are not necessarily connected to many others: While the focal employee on the left

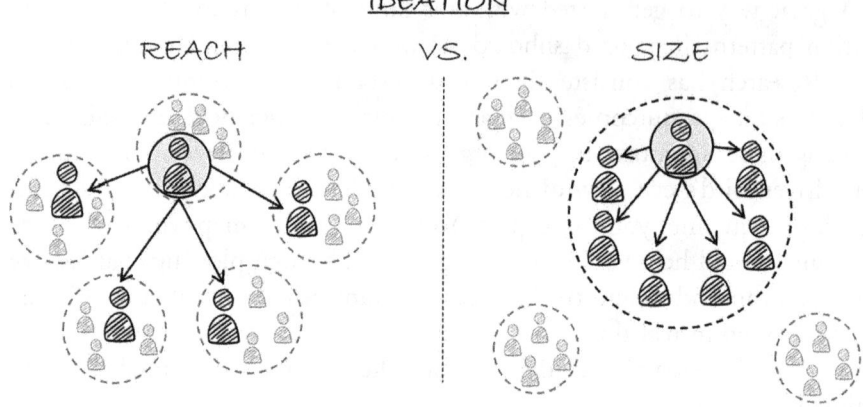

Fig. 2.3 Collaboration signature of ideation

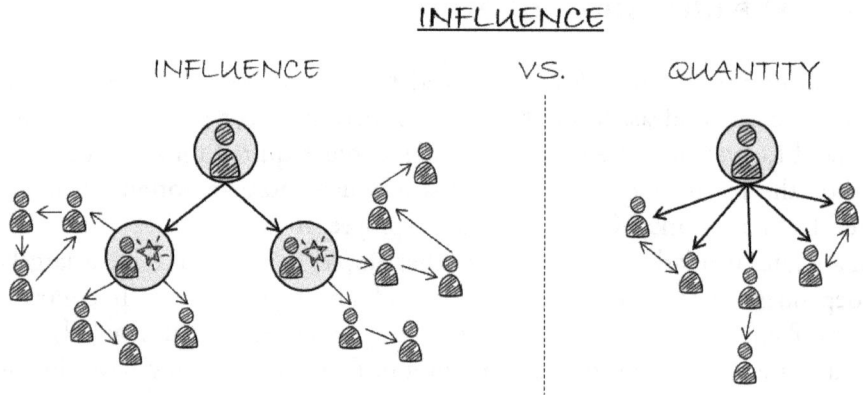

Fig. 2.4 Collaboration signature of influence

side of the panel is connected to fewer colleagues than the focal employee on the right side, she is still more likely to change the behavior of the rest of the group. This is because her connections are themselves better connected.

The core of the influence signature: Having strong connections to influential others.

2.4 The Efficiency Signature

The efficiency signature allows you to identify teams and units that are likely to be good at implementation, will complete projects on time, and excel at execution (Fig. 2.5). Internally, the team members are deeply connected with

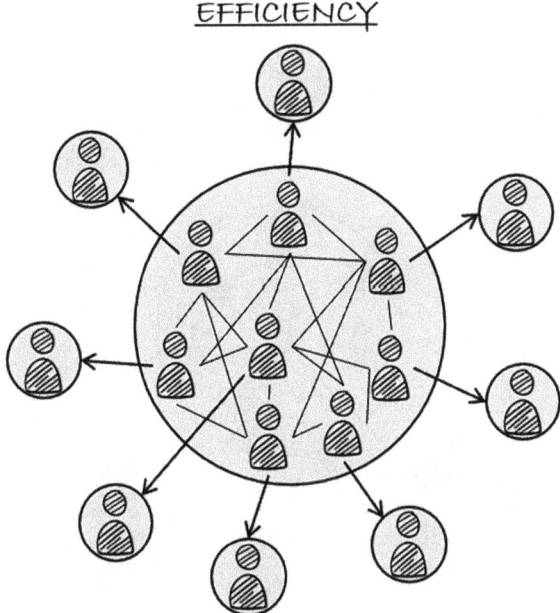

Fig. 2.5 Collaboration signature of efficiency

one another, and the team thus shows high density. This is associated with efficient teamwork. In addition, the team boasts a variety of non-overlapping external contacts, giving them access to helpful and diverse outside resources.

The core of the efficiency signature: High internal connectedness, diverse external connections.

2.5 The Innovation Signature

The innovation signature allows you to identify teams or units that have a high likelihood of innovating effectively (Fig. 2.6). In contrast to the efficiency signature, internal collaborations here are sparser, giving each employee time to develop their own ideas before exposing them to the group. This generally makes for more diverse perspectives and more productive debates. In addition, the team has access to a large range of external collaborators, providing diverse inspiration, flexible informal access to resources, and—if needed—access to political capital that will help them generate buy-in for their innovations.

The core of the innovation signature: Sparse internal connections, diverse external connections.

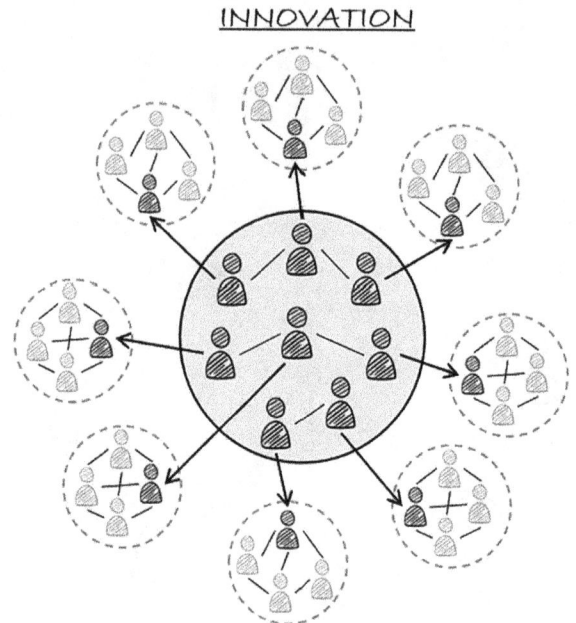

Fig. 2.6 Collaboration signature of innovation

2.6 The Silo Signature

The silo signature allows you to identify units that have a tendency toward group thinking and will be resistant to change (Fig. 2.7). Each team (or department) is intensely connected internally, but connections across team lines are few and far between. As each employee is almost exclusively exposed to peers who share their experiences and social interactions, they, and the team more generally, will form strongly held assumptions about "the right way to do things." Each employee will mostly perceive their own part of the value chain.

The core of the silo signature: Employees have a high ratio of internal to external collaborations.

2.7 The Vulnerability Signature

The vulnerability signature allows you to identify key man risks associated with your interactions with ecosystem partners (Fig. 2.8). It visualizes the degree to which important relationships with strategic suppliers or customers rely on single employees who manage the interfaces. A 1:1 relationship is the

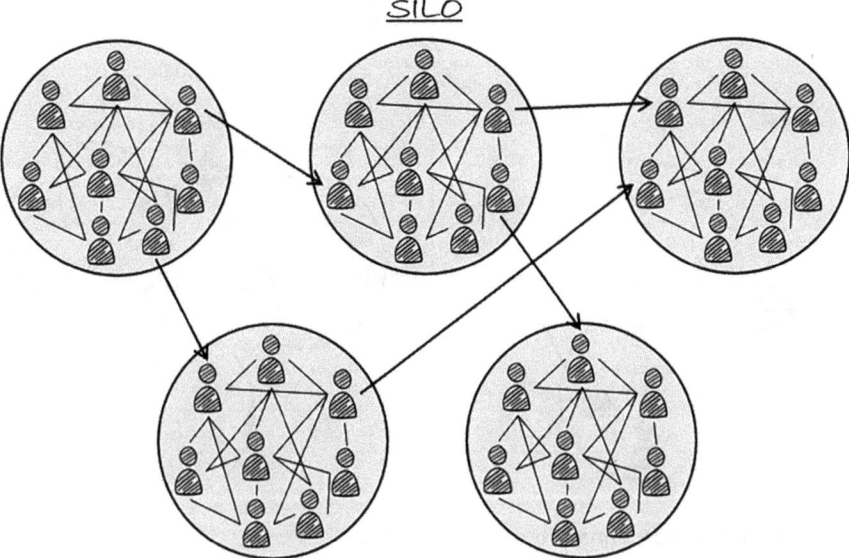

Fig. 2.7 Collaboration signature of silos

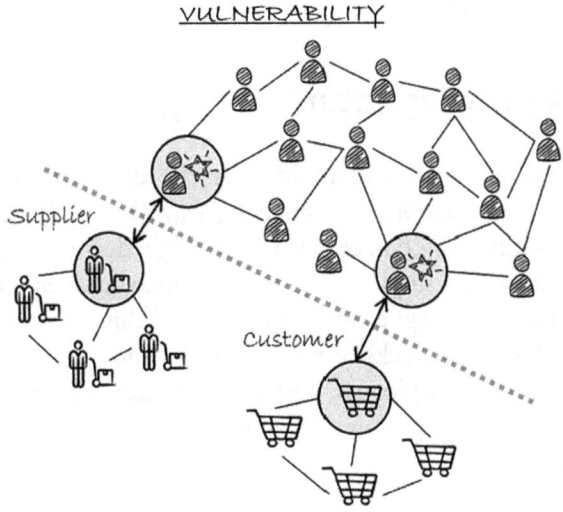

Fig. 2.8 Collaboration signature of vulnerability

most vulnerable, because the departure of any single employee can jeopardize collaboration. The more diversified your contacts at strategic partners, and the less interactions are dominated by a single employee on your end, the more resilient the partnership is to key man risk.

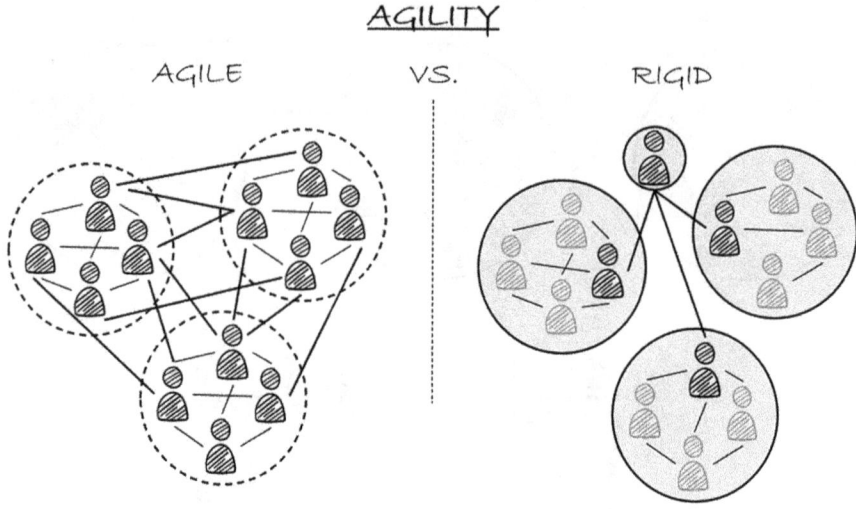

Fig. 2.9 Collaboration signature of agility

The core of the vulnerability signature: Crucial external partnerships managed through a single person-to-person interface.

2.8 The Agility Signature

The agility signature allows you to identify the degree to which units or departments already collaborate in an agile way (Fig. 2.9). Collaborations in rigid organizations are characterized by a high degree of centralization, structural dependency on single employees, distance between employees, and siloed teams. In contrast, agile units generally exhibit a relatively flat social hierarchy, suffer few bottlenecks or redundant collaboration structures, boast short distances between employees, and work in interconnected clusters.

The core of the agility signature: High collaborative intensity between flat and local clusters.

2.9 Culture Analytics Through Digital Footprints

Another digital footprint pervasive in today's business world is language: Employees edit documents, write emails, use message boards, and communicate with customers and external stakeholders. Through all these language artifacts, they leave footprints in which more qualitative aspects of your culture are imprinted: organizational values, identity, approaches to conflict resolution, levels of engagement, and so on.

By analyzing these, you can understand and cluster widely held beliefs and values in your organization. This allows you to assess levels of adoption across units of cultural transformation projects, for example, or observe how a post-merger integration project is progressing.

Some context is necessary in order to interpret this kind of data. Inspired by war stories, many leaders desire strong and cohesive cultures in their organization. But this might be more intuitively appealing than supported by robust evidence. Matthew Corritore, Amir Goldberg, and Sameer Srivastava conducted a series of studies based on more than 500 public companies [2]. They built on the ideas we have outlined here and analyzed language artefacts of the companies' employees to develop data-driven assessments of their cultures. Their key insights:

- Organizations with strong cultures are more profitable, likely driven by the coordinating and energizing effects of intensely held and broadly shared values.
- Organizations with more diverse cultures tend to be more innovative and have faster growth, likely driven by access to more varied perspectives that highlight hard-to-see opportunities.

Much leadership advice (and keynotes on corporate cultures) centers around the idea of aligning your people behind shared values. The benefits of strong cultures, however, come at a cost. The decision to strive toward one should not be a given, but a considered, strategic choice you make for your organization.

2.10 Toward a Data-Driven Future of Leadership?

> The future is here—it is just not equally distributed yet.—William Gibson

Quantifying all these soft factors and taking a data-driven management approach to assessing them might feel unfamiliar at first. As one senior manager told us, "Our supply chain management is an atomic clock, but when it comes to managing our culture, we are a sundial on a foggy day." In our experience, his experience is representative of many organizations: While operational processes are managed in a professional and data-driven way, managerial assessments of the capabilities that really differentiate a company from its competitors are typically based on stories, intuition, and conjecture from low-fidelity data. This doubly applies to the collaboration signatures that enable you to successfully innovate, scale, and transform: Chances are, you don't know how many customer touchpoints your engineers have each quarter or what percentage of time your sales representatives are spending cross-selling to clients from your newly acquired competitor.

When it comes to understanding soft factors, moreover, managerial intuition can be a deceiving guide. The examples of collaboration you see as a senior manager are highly selective, and likely unrepresentative of how the work gets done *on average* in your organization. In most organizations, senior managerial attention is a scarce resource and vied for in intense, behind-the-scenes political processes. Depending on the culture of your organization, what you see will range from the biased to outright staged, but we have yet to see an organization where extrapolating from the personal impressions of senior managers would provide a fair view of typical collaboration practices. Add to this the well-documented array of cognitive and emotional biases humans fall subject to as they attempt to derive persuasive stories from unreliable data, and a need to verify becomes clear. Our recommendation is a healthy dose of skepticism against your own intuitions when it comes to assessing areas like cross-functional collaboration, customer focus, and partner engagement activities.

Today, no one seriously challenges the wisdom of using the latest technology to measure tangible resources, like inventory. What about your organization's most important assets, its intangible resources? Without understanding what goes on in our organizations, we cannot manage them effectively.

As you will see throughout this book, simply building more collaboration interfaces can have negative effects—but by understanding *where* bottlenecks and silos inhibit idea flow, you can create efficient and effective improvements. Understanding collaboration signatures in your organization allows you to gain leverage by pinpointing where interventions yield outsized returns:

- At a consultancy practice with more than 200 employees, the five most-connected leaders were responsible for 40 percent of total revenue [3].

- A medical devices manufacturer found that identifying transformation champions through analytics led to an adoption rate of 75 percent—compared with 15 percent in units that relied on a classical change management approach.
- By targeting and coaching the twenty least efficient collaborators, Monsanto saved up to 1500 work hours per week in their network [4].

By assessing collaboration signatures unobtrusively, you can understand in real time how your transformation is affecting collaboration within your organization. You can double down on what works and know how to change direction if something isn't working. You can identify hidden influencers and optimize your impact. By finding internal silos and disrupting bottlenecks, you can massively increase the flow of ideas and resources through your organization. In essence, you can achieve data-driven management of the often-illusive sources of collaborative advantage.

In recent years, we have seen huge productivity increases through the adoption of data-driven optimization in the realm of tangible resources. The smart enterprise today uses real-time enterprise resource planning (ERP) and optimizes supply chains, pricing, marketing, and production processes through data.

But competition is no longer primarily based on organizations' tangible resources, and we see the potential for a similar revolution in the field of intangible resources, such as culture, the ability to innovate, and customer retention. These represent a growing share of companies' valuations. And while these areas used to be the realm of intuitive judgments and gut feeling, AI-enabled analytics will increasingly support data-driven decision-making:

We are already seeing the pioneers push ahead: According to a recent survey, the most successful companies are thirteen times more likely to apply this kind of analytics [5] (Fig. 2.10). By getting real-time insights into the "oft side" of their organizations, they disrupt bottlenecks, connect silos, and drive value-added collaboration.

Given these facts, just one question remains: Is your organization ready for a data-driven approach to the human side of transformation?

2.11 The Next Step

If you want to explore this potential for your organization, go to collaborative-advantage.org/analytics for suggestions and resources on how to get started. Among others, you will find:

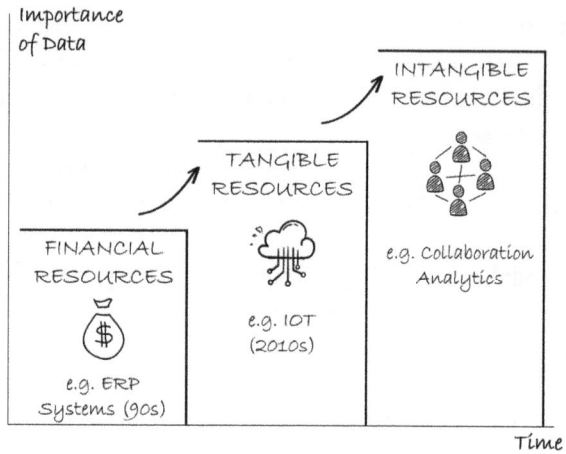

Fig. 2.10 Data-driven management of intangible resources

- A one-hour sample workshop on how to discuss these ideas with your relevant stakeholders (complete with agenda, a pre-read, suggested slides, and outcomes).
- A step-by-step guide for how to conduct this kind of analysis.
- Use cases and ideas for action on how to use generative AI such as ChatGPT in people analytics to drive collaborative advantage—constantly updated in response to the rapid pace of technological change.

You can also scan the QR Code if you don't like typing. The resources are completely free.

References

In order to keep the book lean enough to comfortably be read on a plane, we have listed the full references on the companion website for your convenience. If you want to dig deeper, please check them out here:

1. Collaborative-advantage.org/references-analytics/1.
2. Collaborative-advantage.org/references-analytics/2.
3. Collaborative-advantage.org/references-analytics/3.
4. Collaborative-advantage.org/references-analytics/4.
5. Collaborative-advantage.org/references-analytics/5.

Part II

Collaborative Innovation

3

Dynamics of Collaborative Innovation

Innovation distinguishes between a leader and a follower.
—Steve Jobs

3.1 Co-create Your Future Business with Customers

"I have good news and bad news." When he first heard these words from one of his key account managers, Marco Meyrat had no idea they would set him on a course to radically transform his company. Indeed, the former general manager of Hilti Switzerland doesn't look or sound like a radical innovator at first sight. He wears frameless glasses, and for our interview had chosen a meticulous gray suit. In precise, slightly Swiss-inflected English, he told us about his company's transformation journey slowly and analytically, demonstrating nearly encyclopedic recollection. In other words, he comes off more as an administrator than revolutionary. And yet, after his talk with the key account manager, he would go on to radically rewrite the DNA of his company. The headline for this change: Fleet Management.

Meyrat drove a renewal process that saw Hilti go from being a commodity product manufacturer to a global high-end service provider. He completely altered the strategic positioning of the company, landing it in a differentiated and thus profitable position. Fleet management came to represent about 60 percent of top line revenue in key markets and was profitable than legacy offerings. As Hilti's chief technology officer later put it: "Hilti developed many very innovative and successful products over the years, but they paled in comparison to the fleet management business model, which was the most important innovation in Hilti's history."

Of course, going into that foundational meeting, neither Marco Meyrat nor his key account manager was aware that they were about change the course of the company's history. Instead, their focus is narrow: attracting and retaining a particular customer. The sales rep had just closed a new, big contract with Batigroup, then the largest construction company in Switzerland. This was the good news. The bad news was that Batigroup had requested a holistic tool management system. They wanted to outsource finance, maintenance, administrative activities, and more to Hilti. In other words, they wanted Hilti to enter the fleet management market.

This was not exactly a logical next step in Hilti's offering. The Liechtenstein-based multinational was one of the world's largest manufacturers of power tools in the premium segment. Its strengths were the quality of its products, technological innovation, and a large, efficient sales force that allowed the company to sell its tools directly to customers at construction sites rather than via the retailers on whom its competitors depended. When Meyrat told his boss, chief executive Pius Baschera, about Batigroup's proposal Baschera's concerns thus were palpable. It "implies a radical break from Hilti's current business methods," he pointed out, and argued there was no urgent need to abandon "our tried-and-true methods." The shift "represents a high risk for Hilti," he told Meyrat.

Despite these reservations, the company's board gave Meyrat the go-ahead to try and develop a new offering based on Batigroup's request. He did so in stages, starting with a co-development with seven pilot customers in Switzerland with whom Hilti had strong existing relationships. Based on this experience, a package, which was now being called Fleet, was offered to the whole of the relatively small Swiss market. It was then extended to the German market—a substantially bigger testing ground, but still largely familiar. Finally, Hilti rolled out Fleet globally. In Marco Meyrat's recollection, this iterative approach, which allowed Hilti to learn and successively rise to new challenges, was crucial to the eventual success of the solution: "If we would have launched globally right from the beginning, we wouldn't be where we are today."

> **Lesson Learned:**
>
> Hilti's four iterative steps to success:
>
> 1. Piloting with existing customers
> 2. Roll-out in small Swiss market
> 3. Extension to German market
> 4. Global roll-out

Starting small allowed the company to use lean solutions, avoid complex processes, and capitalize on an engaged and focused core team in the beginning to build early success stories with pilot customers. For example, early fleet management was essentially managed using Excel sheets rather than building new software. Once the solution started gaining traction, the company had to make a decision: Did they want a business that could move the needle for Hilti by creating material revenue growth or was this going to be a nice little lighthouse project mostly useful for marketing purposes? Choosing to scale the new offering meant huge changes for Hilti itself.

For example, the financial management of the company had been optimized for product transactions in which revenues were realized in one go, at point of sale. Fleet introduced a recurring revenue structure with monthly billables. In addition, the tools were often financed by Hilti, which meant customers in effect received loans from the group. All of these changes created a huge disruption in cash-flow patterns.

The legal department at Hilti was also affected. At the start of Fleet, they were issuing long and complex contracts to customers that were often a serious impediment to completing the sale. "Buying a plane was easier than buying fleet management from Hilti," Meyrat joked. With some focused management, the contracts were brought down from almost fifty pages to one double-sided sheet.

But the scope of the transformation is best seen in the way Hilti sold its new services.

Hilti was always an incredibly sales driven organization. New hires in their prestigious outperformer program have to start in direct sales for a full year before transitioning to management roles. The company tracks daily customer contacts as an important KPI (~250.000 throughout the organization). And three in four employees are regular direct contact with customers. The primacy of sales nurtures a culture of customer empathy and customer centricity across the organization.

For the sales organization, the transformation from selling individual power tools to selling fleet management was incredibly challenging.

First, the buyer changed—from the foreman at a construction site to senior management at a buying center. As such, the salespeople's old go-to resources became irrelevant. They had long relied on live demonstrations of technologically superior Hilti tools; these made more sense at building sites than boardrooms. They had also made good use of the pricing flexibility that goes hand-in-hand with relatively opaque one-to-one negotiations; this disappeared with fundamentally consistent contracts. As such, Hilti's core department needed to undergo a huge change in culture, away from transactional sales and toward a consultative model of sales. This meant helping customers to use the fleet management *solution*, coaching them, for example, in how to include it in their business processes and or roll it out across their program. In addition, the physics of recurring revenue models necessitated a radical shift toward customer success management: Gone were the days when salespeople could sell a product, shake a hand, and disappear until the next sale season. Instead, aftersales relationship management and customer enablement increased in relative importance. In order to earn contract renewals and expansions, Hilti salespeople had to stay engaged with their partners and consistently demonstrate and redemonstrate the value of their solution [1].

Hilti's experience is representative of a modern, collaborative approach to innovation. Fleet management started with an idea from a customer, not from Hilti. Rather than merely asking for the "faster horses" of Henry Ford lore, customers can drive transformative innovation. Hilti, in turn, was open enough to realize the potential behind this request and flexible enough to sharpen and co-create the offering with a focus group of strategic partners. This collaborative approach is quickly emerging as the new North tar for innovation leaders—and it is not limited to customer-driven innovation. Consider how Airbus develops future technologies through supplier innovation days. Henkel, the German chemicals giant, cranks up the pressure by ending relationships with suppliers that are not able to consistently innovate to keep up with ambitious improvement targets. Mammut, the Swiss mountaineering brand, extends this approach beyond direct partners: Its water repellent zipping mechanism for outdoor jackets was developed through a crowd-intelligence platform.

This emerging collaborative approach to innovation replaces the closed R&D units of the past with an open flow of ideas and inspiration up and down the value chain: "The lab is our world" becomes "the world is our lab." Collaboration enables an outside-in perspective by using the creative potential of suppliers, high-tech companies, outsourcing partners, strategic alliances, and even the crowd to create new offerings.

Quick Win:

Listen to your customers—they might have an idea to successfully innovate and transform your business, unlocking unknown potential. Make a habit of trying to learn something every time you have a customer interaction. For instance, try the following:

- In the next meeting with one of your customers, use the initial small talk to ask discovery questions such as: What is your number one challenge at the moment? Tell me about the last time you had a big frustration with our product? What would our product need to do additionally for you to be happy to pay double for it? What do you dream of?
- During innovation projects, challenge your teams to involve real customers much earlier than they would normally. Google Sprints, for example, require direct customer interaction just four days after work on a project has started.
- Initiate lead-user workshops: Invite opinion leaders and your most demanding customers to a workshop with your R&D team. Hilti regularly holds workshops and reaps huge gains in terms of innovation, including the invention of a whole new division focused on measurement.

3.2 Break Up Internal Echo Chambers to Drive Idea Flow

The Israeli financial services company eToro allows individual investors to trade securities and other asset classes. That doesn't exactly sound unique. But unlike other online platforms, eToro incentivizes traders to make their positions and trades public. This allows other traders to emulate the most successful traders' strategies. And because it happens on a digital platform, it provides a real-life terrarium to observe the pattern of information sharing, collaboration, and social learning. In other words, we have a digital footprint of the collaborative signatures of the trading network. By analyzing this data [2], we can understand how interacting with and learning from other traders influences investment decision-making, uncertainty management, and traders' ability to adapt to change.

Self-Reflection:

Take a step back and think about what you would expect: How important are the traders' social interactions to their performance? And which group of traders will perform best: The ones with many connections or the ones with few?

The returns investors achieve are strongly predicted by their social connections to other traders on the platform: Some traders are isolated. They don't follow many other traders, and mostly do their own thing. These traders achieved results that were, on average, slightly below those of a standard market index. Traders with a moderately greater number of social connections were substantially more successful: They learned from well-performing traders, had early access to superior information and strategies, and were able to earn a full 35 percent premium over the overall market results.

These results might not seem terribly surprising. It is not just the direction of the effect, but its strength that is worth noting. It shows how important collaboration is for sensing investment opportunities. Being informally exposed to successful traders allows individuals to learn the best strategies for competing and spotting competitive changes ahead of the overall market. Just by seeing with whom and how often a trader interacts, we can make a good estimate of their overall profitability. As we will see, this also holds true for understanding how well employees and teams within organizations are able to sense innovative opportunities creatively.

The story gets even more interesting, moreover, when we look at a final group of traders the most connected. You might think that if more connections are better, having the most connections would be the best. You'd be wrong. It turns out traders with very high levels of social connections performed worst.

Why? It turns out that, when it comes to the impact of social exchanges on managing uncertainty, quality matters more than quantity.

Over time, the highly connected traders formed echo chambers with other investors. While they felt they were following many different people and learning from a diverse set of strategies, everyone was following each other one another. As in a game of Chinese whispers, the same suboptimal trading strategies were passed around by traders who wrongly believed the strategy had been validated by a variety of different investors, all independently reaching the same conclusions.

The impact was most negative in the face of discontinuous change—whether that was a bubble bursting in the securities market, a disruptive new technology, or a surprising customer trend. Closely connected echo chambers are exceptionally rigid. Like in a perpetual motion machine, the rigid and siloed collaboration signature in this environment keeps the investors on course.

We observe similar structures in many companies that fail to adapt to disruptive change: A rigidity enabled by overly strong managerial social connections in closed circles within companies or industries.

> **Lesson Learned:**
> Having the right connections (not the most!) and collaborating with experts (also externally!) are important indicators for successful innovation, as this connectedness creates valuable learning possibilities. But be careful: If the collaboration network gets too large and homogeneous, you might lose the flexibility to adapt to change, counteracting innovation.

A platform like eToro's, which combines trading with social networking, allows us to experiment in ways that are often impossible in organizations. The researchers decided to break up the overly interconnected echo chambers to determine if financial decision-making could be improved. They did this by simultaneously decreasing the intensity of social connections within the echo chambers and introducing new, more diverse perspectives. Changes to eToro's structure let them decrease the frequency of interactions and updates between highly connected traders. At the same time, central traders who were followed by many other traders were encouraged using financial incentives to observe and mirror strategies from successful traders outside of their social circle—those who used to be more isolated.

Through these changes, many of the most rigid echo chambers in the network were disrupted. This had a profound effect on how well traders were able to manage the stock market's uncertainty and volatility: Over the entire network, profitability *doubled* after the intervention.

We stated earlier that understanding the pattern of social interactions—or the collaboration signatures—of an individual trader allows us to make a fairly accurate estimate of his ability to spot investment opportunities. The truth, it turns out, is far more exciting: We can use this knowledge to *change* traders' ability to spot investment opportunities. By actively managing the collaborations of the investment network, the researchers increased profitability to a degree that would be absolutely transformative for most businesses. The users of eToro didn't learn new technical skills about options pricing; no investment tips were shared or other tangible resources distributed; from the perspective of the individual trader, nothing changed.

But behind the curtain, in the pattern of social interactions we call collaboration signatures, a few tweaks to an algorithm changed the trading network's fortunes.

> **Self-Reflection:**
> Does your organization suffer from the existence of echo chambers? Find out by answering these three questions:
>
> 1. Are your employees strongly interconnected within their teams but not across other teams?
> 2. Do you have long-lasting working groups with little or no fluctuation of members?
> 3. Do your employees have similar backgrounds or are they part of similar social circles?
> 4. Is there a lack of outside perspective in your teams?
>
> If you've answered yes to any of these questions, then your organization may well be stymied by echo chambers. Your team may reject outside ideas out of hand—a condition known as "not invented here" (NIH) syndrome. The more stable the working constellations, the more acute the syndrome. Fortunately, we have some advice for cracking these echo chambers.

3.3 Use Leadership Incentives to Nurture Innovation Across Silos

How can managers ensure that echo chambers do not make their teams blind to lucrative new opportunities? Consider the example of Bridgewater Associates. Founded in 1975 by Ray Dalio out of his New York apartment, the company is now the largest hedge fund globally and, according to Fortune magazine, the fifth most important private company in the world. This ascent was largely powered by the company's ability to spot investment opportunities in times of disruptive change long before market consensus followed suit. For example, Bridgewater foresaw the global financial crisis of 2008 and not only repositioned their portfolio but also warned the White House Treasury about the impending crash (alas, to no avail). As a journalist for Barron's wrote, "nobody was better prepared for the global market crash" than Bridgewater clients. Behind this success lies an almost obsessive focus on making investment decisions in an "idea meritocracy," a context where the best ideas win instead of the ones most favored in closed echo chambers of senior decision-makers. In order to achieve this, the company focuses on radical transparency and an explicit model of gathering and analyzing assessments of its employees [3].

Let's look at how this works in practice and join the research team a week after the 2016 election of Donald Trump as they try to determine the implications for the US economy. Naturally, people have different opinions, so Bridgewater uses a tool they call the "Dot Collector." The collector lets team members input their opinions into a shared dashboard, and provides a constant stream of peer feedback to colleagues. For example, in that November 2016 meeting, Jen, a 24-year-old recent college graduate, responded to questions about team members' approaches to the prediction exercises by rating Bridgewater's chief executive, who was in attendance, a three on a 1–10 scale. He did not demonstrate a good balance of assertiveness and open-mindedness, she said. Over time, assessments like these allow the decision-makers to visualize the landscape of opinions beyond their closed personal interactions. They can contextualize their own assessments as one of many by seeing the many on the shared dashboard. They start asking themselves, "How do I know my opinion is right? Have we considered all perspectives? What are contrarian positions, and what are they based upon?".

The Dot Collector observes how people think and notes correlations. Guided by algorithms, it can provide feedback on whether individuals are seeing a sufficient number of different perspectives suggest working partners based on complementary strengths or different views. Over time, it develops a quantitative assessment of the believability of the employee's assessments in a variety of areas and uses this to pool relevant assessments across the whole network rather than just within the tribal echo chambers of senior decision-makers. It extends social learning beyond the close personal connections people tend to build and maintain among people like themselves, and challenges rigid assumptions predominant in echo chambers. In the words of Ray Dalio: "We do it because it elevates ourselves above our own opinions so that we start to see things through everybody's eyes, and we see things collectively. Collective decision-making is so much better than individual decision-making if it's done well. It's been the secret sauce behind our success. It's why we've made more money for our clients than any other hedge fund in existence and made money twenty-three out of the last twenty-six years."

> **Lesson Learned:**
> Opinions from employees across your company, independent of seniority, and from your customers, are required for collective decision-making and finding the best idea.

> *Don't overinvest in an idea before conducting and internal and external validation!*
> So the next time you have to make an important decision or need inspiration, share the challenge across your organization, and ask for input. Maybe one of your employees has exactly the idea you need. Think, too, about external collaborations and co-workings with customers to bring in new perspectives.

While a data-driven strategy is certainly the most effective way to alleviate the negative implications of overly rigid internal echo chambers, organizations have developed broader, intuition-based approaches as well. For example, some of the most innovative organizations run short-term cross-functional collaboration "sprints" such as Facebook's "Hackamonth," which developed central features of Facebook's business, including the "like" button and Messenger. Other organizations strive to alleviate rigid and unquestioned structures by rotating staff regularly.

When was the last time you had an intimate understanding of a crucial business challenge outside of your own reporting line? Hilti recognized the need to enable its employees to form deep, value-added relationships across departments through its Outperformer program. In that first year of sales, they develop an intimate understanding of their end customers: What are the key struggles of construction workers, how do they collaborate and make decisions? How is the value of Hilti's products felt in their everyday life? As we will see in many examples throughout the book, cultivating rich and diverse external interfaces is key for organizations to sense innovative opportunities, seize them with customer-centric offerings, and energize transformations as the competitive landscape changes.

In addition, Outperformer participants get to know Hilti's permanent salespeople, and the inhabitants of other customer-facing departments. What drives them? What keeps them from going the extra mile? They take knowledge with them to whichever department they eventually land. To avoid not just functional but regional silos, Hilti also makes sure their Outperformers spend six months in the local headquarters, and that they do at least some training at the global headquarters in Liechtenstein. And they do a three-month rotation abroad. These experiences mean program participants can eventually build on diverse, boundary-spanning personal relations that allow them to quickly access ideas, feedback, and resources from across the entire organization. They get internal and external insights in different regions, from different functions of the company.

Other companies have developed leaner approaches to nurture these direct customer interfaces. The financial services company Stripe, for example, has its engineers rotate between product development and customer support. While not uniformly loved by the engineers at first, the policy created much more empathy for how (often unsophisticated) customers, and a better understanding of how they interact with Stripe's products; this has inspired more customer-centric product design.

If implemented at scale, such initiatives offer fairly simple actionable angles for managers to nurture boundary-spanning personal relationships in a critical mass of high-potential employees—and thus reduce the risk of echo chambers blinding their strategic decision-making.

> **Quick Win:**
> Your next meeting with senior decision-makers provides the opportunity for a simple assessment.
>
> - Before the meeting, seek out some less connected employees and ask for their opinions on a few critical points to be discussed.
> - For example, before making an acquisition decision, you could ask about the likely future of the core technologies the acquisition target relies upon, how demand for the type of service the target provides will likely develop in the next years, and how your company is positioned to capture a relevant share of this market.
> - As you engage in the meeting, compare the estimations of your senior decision-makers with the estimations of the more isolated employees you talked to ahead of time. If the opinions of your senior management team are mostly just a more-confident version of the consensus of the more isolated employees, the danger is high that you are in an echo chamber and would profit from being challenged by more independent outside voices.

Let's say an echo chamber structure characterizes your organization. Are there ways to correct this in your decision-making? There are, and most rely on a more structured approach to informing and documenting the basis for your decision-making. A key skill here is to identify contrarians in your organizations. Who are the people in your organization who tend to disagree with the majority's opinion? Who behaves differently than the rest, especially without obvious cause? These are people connected to the rest of their tribe but who are willing to run counter to the social consensus. For example, a local business unit leader might follow a different sales approach than the rest of the organization. Since these contrarian thinkers have access to the social consensus on how their business should be managed and still decide to go against this consensus, they likely have access to independent information and high confidence in this information. Of course, they just might be wrong. This is why a key part of this strategy is to keep monitoring these independent, contrarian thinkers in your organization and watch out for situations where a consensus emerges among these more independent thinkers that runs counter to the organization's overall consensus. These independent consensus opinions will often help you identify investment opportunities that might have gone unnoticed. In the eToro example, the consensus of these independent thinkers' trading strategies was reliably *more than twice as good as the best individual human trader.*

> **Lesson Learned:**
>
> How to avoid overly rigid internal echo chambers:
>
> - Develop temporary cross-functional collaboration formats.
> - Set up internal rotation programs, so employees experience different departments.
> - Send employees to different geographical regions, expose them to different contexts.
> - Pay attention to the contrarians/independent thinkers in your organization.
> - Increase external collaborations with start-ups, customers, etc.

3.4 Understand the Benefits of Social Learning

Why are social connections so crucial to adaptability and the ability to learn, such that a relatively simple change can yield huge benefits? Humans discover, develop, and validate new ideas through social interaction. The myth of the lone, brilliant inventor in his garage is mostly just that—a myth. In reality, innovation is a group endeavor that builds on smart ways to recombine existing knowledge and capabilities. As Steve Jobs put it, "Creativity is just connecting things. When you ask creative people how they did something, they feel a little guilty because they didn't really do it—they just saw something." But how often do we connect things that haven't yet been connected by our competitors?

Organizations differ to a huge degree in how well they are able to nurture these types of connections. In some organizations, there are simply not enough opportunities to connect. In others, there are many connections, but not necessarily between the right employees. But again and again, we have found the same basic pattern behind the innovative output and the adaptability of a huge variety of organizations. And this fundamental relationship seems to explain more than just organizational innovation. For example, we can predict the GDP growth and creative output of entire cities based on GPS data modeling of personal interactions between members of different neighborhoods—or put differently, by understanding the collaboration signatures within cities, we can predict which will thrive [4].

That humans are so incredibly dependent on social learning, and that we build creative solutions on the shoulders of existing knowledge, is not a defect. Research shows that in complex environments, the optimal learning strategy is to spend *90 percent of your time and resources on social learning*, which is to say, finding and mirroring others who perform well, and only 10 percent on individual reflection [5]. The collaboration signatures of organizations show whom your employees are learning from, and whether they are hitting that ideal 90 percent social learning mark.

> **Self-Reflection:**
> When faced with a complex challenge, how much time do you spend seeking out others to learn from and how much do you try to come up with a solution yourself?

3.5 Build a Culture of Creative Collisions

Are creative collisions a matter of luck? Or can you design your organization to systematically produce them?

To see an organization actively designing for these collisions, look no further than W.L. Gore & Associates, the manufacturer most famous for the invention of Gore-Tex fabric. The founder, Bill Gore, built his organization on Douglas McGregor's positive view of humanity. Gore was convinced that the right leadership style was "freedom and commitment" rather than "command and control." For this reason, his company is organized very differently from most. He calls the construct a "lattice organization," and it functions more like a network than a hierarchy. Everyone has the opportunity to communicate with everyone else. The company has managed to systematically create creative collisions by nurturing collaborations that span internal boundaries. This structure also makes room for winding career paths and supports work done predominantly in teams.

Within Gore, employees are not assigned to specific projects. Instead, they are encouraged to work on the projects where they see their skills best fitting.

And if someone has an idea for a project, they can pursue it as soon as they find two other people with the right skills to join them. This means no formal approval process, just peer-coordination to filter and develop innovative ideas. This spirit is also manifested in a policy that provides employees with the right to use 10 percent of their time to explore new ideas and initiatives (similar to policies at other innovation leaders such as 3M or Google).

This bold approach to enabling collaborative, rather than formal, decision-making in matters of innovation explains how mountain bikes and dental floss came together at Gore to create market-leading guitar strings [6]: Dave Myers, a passionate mountain biker, worked in a Gore medical device plant developing new types of heart implants. In his dabbling time, he decided to do something close to his heart and try to improve his mountain bike by coating his gear cables with a layer of plastic. His goal was to make the gears shift more smoothly. After some successful experimentation, he wanted to do more with his findings. He thought of using a similar coating of plastic on guitar strings to improve their feel and durability. Since he was not a guitar player himself, he sought help from a coworker. The duo experimented for a bit but were not satisfied with the outcome. They reached out through their informal, personal network to an engineer named John Spencer for some help. Spencer had some expertise in the field of dental floss and brought in another perspective and skill set; soon after they started to work together, they were able to present a viable product, seek official sponsorship from Gore, and take their strings to the market. Elixir guitar strings were a wild success. Eight years after launch, they commanded more than a third of market share.

Gore did away not only with predefined work groups, but with traditional titles. Experienced organization members are dubbed sponsors, recognizing the importance of strong relationships between employees. Every new associate is assigned a starting sponsor. The sponsor's job is to connect the new hire with others in the firm. As Donna Frey, the former head of HR describes, "We encourage the new hire to meet with these associates one-on-one. It's not a phone conversation, but a chance to sit down with them face-to-face and get to know them." By creating a list with key associates they should meet, sponsors create for the new hires a network.

"When you're hiring really good people, they want to have quick wins and make contributions," says Frey. "Building relationships without a clear goal can be difficult. Often, new associates will say, 'I don't feel like I'm contributing. I've spent three months just getting to know people.' However, after a year they begin to realize how important this process was."

> **Lesson Learned:**
> Transformative innovations are created in organizations that actively manage collaborations where diverse perspectives can effortlessly collide. It's not about teamwork or inspiration from other fields. It's also not about connecting many people, it's about connecting the right people in the right way. And, at scale, it is about building an organization which achieves that *all the time*.

Author Daniele Coyle shared an anecdote that illustrates this process of creating revolutionary innovation step-by-step [7]:

Today, Google is admired as one of the world's most innovative organizations. But in the early 2000s, it was far from clear that this would be the case. In fact, a company called Overture was the clear frontrunner in the race to dominate internet advertising. Led by Bill T. Gross, an entrepreneur who had essentially invented internet advertising and the pay-per-click model, Overture was a thriving, profitable business that attracted a (given the times) rather eye-watering valuation of 1 billion dollars for a largely asset-free business. In contrast, Google was still a fledgling start-up struggling to deliver relevant ads with its core technology. For example, if a user searched for Kawasaki H1B motorcycles, he would see a "targeted" advertisement from lawyers offering help with H1B Visa applications. Frustrated, Google founder Larry Page printed several particularly egregious examples and pinned them in the company kitchen together with a note: These Ads Suck.

As it turned out, Google was in possession of the necessary knowledge to creatively solve this challenge. Unfortunately, as happens so often in organizations, the knowledge required for the solution did not reside where the knowledge of the challenge sat (better not mention incentives). But this was about to change: One of the engineers to spot Page's note was Jeff Dean, a software engineer working in a completely different area of the company. While making himself a cappuccino, Dean skimmed through the note's attachments and remembered a similar problem he dealt with a while back. Without asking for permission or telling anyone, the engineer started to work on the problem. He stayed over the weekend, and finally sent his solution to the team on Monday morning at 5:05 a.m. Exhausted, he went to bed.

Dean's fix worked and boosted the recommendation's accuracy. After adopting it, Google's AdWords profits surged from $6 million to $99 million; today advertising accounts for 90 percent of Google's revenues. Overture couldn't keep up and was sold to Yahoo. Author Stephen Levy described the success of the AdWords engine as "sudden, transformative, decisive and, for Google's inventors and employees, glorious… It became the lifeblood of

Google, funding every new idea and innovation the company conceived of thereafter."

Most interesting for our collaborative perspective on innovation, however, is the epilogue to this anecdote. Google advisor Jonathan Rosenberg interviewed Jeff Dean about his solution in 2013. Rosenberg expected Dean to reminisce at length about this masterstroke. But Dean barely recalled what he was talking about. "I mean, I remember that it happened," Dean later told author Daniele Coyle. "But to be completely honest, it didn't register strongly in my memory because it didn't feel like that big of a deal. It didn't feel special or different. It was normal. That kind of thing happened all the time."

It was normal—that kind of thing happened all the time. This is where the anecdote stops being about Jeff Dean and starts being about Google and its collaborative advantage: an environment where knowledge and skills flow so freely through the organization that a moment like this barely registers. As at Gore, people with different skill sets are mixed and remixed, creating a deep and diverse network of personal relationships. Consequently, employees such as Dave Myers know somebody (who knows somebody) who has the skillset to bring a transformative new perspective to their project—and they can energize their colleague's commitment to their project through a network of personal bonds.

> **Self-Reflection:**
> Do knowledge and skills flow freely through your organization? Is collaboration between people with different abilities fostered? Do employees have a network throughout the entire organization?

> **Quick Win:**
> If you tend to answer these questions with a "no," try the following:
>
> - Establish monthly knowledge-exchange roundtables, where people of one team/department present a project they're currently working on in order to obtain feedback from other teams/departments on a specific question they have or problems they face.
> - Create an "Innovation Board" with employees from your organization but also external experts to bring in new perspectives and jointly develop innovative solutions.

- Start "speed dating" projects around strategic topics (and also invite start-ups, partners, and customers to take part).

References

In order to keep the book lean enough to comfortably be read on a plane, we have listed the full references on the companion website for your convenience. If you want to dig deeper, please check them out here:

1. Collaborative-advantage.org/references-innovation/1.
2. Collaborative-advantage.org/references-innovation/2.
3. Collaborative-advantage.org/references-innovation/3.
4. Collaborative-advantage.org/references-innovation/4.
5. Collaborative-advantage.org/references-innovation/5.
6. Collaborative-advantage.org/references-innovation/6.
7. Collaborative-advantage.org/references-innovation/7.

4

Leading for Collaborative Innovation

I not only use all the brains I have, but all that I can borrow.
—Woodrow Wilson

4.1 Lead for Collisions, Not for More Meetings

Reducing social connections to increase the adaptivity of groups, as in the eToro example, is not the sort of recommendation you'll find in many management books. So what does our collaborative view of organizations say about how managers might get better at sensing innovative opportunities?

Science writer Steven Johnson summarizes his analysis of some of the most important and consequential scientific inventions and breakthroughs of history as follows [8]: "If you look at history, innovation doesn't come just from giving people incentives; it comes from environments where their ideas can connect." Based on our own work, we would amend this statement: Innovation comes from an environment where *diverse* ideas can connect. The degree to which this is enabled or inhibited is largely determined by the collaboration signatures of the organization.

Many managers feel they have access to diverse perspectives and a range of relevant viewpoints because they talk to many different people. If there is a lot of communication going on in their organization, surely new ideas must regularly emerge from these connections? However, to understand the collaborative approach to innovation, the relevant question is not "How many people do I talk to?" but "How many people do I talk to *who otherwise do not speak to one another*?" Or, "How many people do I talk to who are different from me in some fundamental way?".

> **Self-Reflection:**
> - What is the effective size of your collaborative reach?
> - Or put differently, how many different groups are you exposed to who think independently from each other about similar issues?
>
> If you tend to collaborate only with people in a closed circle, try to increase your collaborative reach by deliberately looking for an exchange with someone who is working on similar topics but is not part of this closed circle.
>   Then, over lunch or coffee, get a new perspective on the topics you're working on. It will probably benefit both of you.

Members of Raphael's research group back at the Rotterdam School of Management looked at this dynamic in a multinational asset management fund. As most managers can attest, even within departments employees tend to form cliques that communicate and collaborate a lot internally, and significantly less so with members from other cliques. In adaptive organizations, these cliques are connected like neighborhoods in a city through various collaboration highways; in less adaptive companies, they can evolve into largely separated silos. Raphael's former colleagues wanted to determine whether the collaborations connecting these cliques could predict which of the fund's highly skilled employees would be the most innovative.

The results were striking: Collaborative reach into diverse groups that had otherwise limited connections to one another was necessary for innovativeness.

> **Lesson Learned:**
> There was not a single highly innovative employee who did not collaborate with otherwise separated cliques to an unusually high degree.

Creative opportunities are often uncovered in a clash of diverse perspectives. Historically, many innovation centers have been cultural melting pots where diverse cultures and tribes collide.

Many companies today follow 3M's example of building a platform dedicated to the internal exchange of ideas. In 2008, in the depths of the global economic downturn, 3M launched its first innovation platform, "InnovationLive." It attracted the engagement of 1300 employees in more than 40 countries, with the goal of developing new ideas for gaining market share. Similar initiatives can now be found at Dell, with its Ideastorm platform, and P&G, where all innovation leads are stored in one location accessible to all employees. At Swisscom, a Swiss telecoms provider, every employee is able to put ideas forward in their Kickbox program. If accepted, the company provides some funding, time, written advice, and support from innovation experts. Programs like these are especially valuable if they generate more reach for their innovation process, meaning more people have the opportunity to share their ideas. The process needs to be fast and fuss-free. Other companies engage in face-to-face exchange and offer events to share experiences and ideas, such as the TEDxJNJ talks at Johnson & Johnson or Brown Bag Lunches organized by HP.

> *Leader's voice: Creating partnerships for innovation at Google.*
>
> *For companies struggling to innovate, the idea of innovating in an ecosystem with external partners might be easy to accept. But what about at a company with a history of innovative success, which sees itself as the disruptor rather than the disrupted? John Hennessey, chairman of Alphabet (formerly Google), is curious, enthusiastic, and eminently knowledgeable about a wide range of topics. During our interview, he explained his approach to this challenge by describing a crucial pivot at Google: the acquisition of YouTube. As an up-and-coming service with no steady revenue model, it wasn't exactly clear that YouTube would prove to be a winner. Even more important, Google had launched its own service, Google Video, which was directly competing with YouTube.*
>
> *Hennessey argues that getting the management buy-in to overcome not-invented-here syndrome is often a question of finding the right way to frame the decision. In the case of YouTube, the acquisition was not done on the basis of technical analyses (although plenty of those were undertaken). Instead, the watershed moment was a single remark in private discussion with the founders of YouTube: "Video is to the next generation what email is to your generation." After thinking about the acquisition from this frame, the decision was essentially made.*
>
> *As for managing internal overlaps, Hennessey explained that, after the acquisition, Google celebrated the internal coopetition to spark more radical innovation: "In such cases, whether it was Google Video versus YouTube or Google Music versus YouTube Music, we were letting them run in parallel to see how they were growing." At the same time, shared technology stacks (particularly*

> *machine learning facilities) ensured cross-fertilization across these competing initiatives.*
>
> *In the end, "the purchase price of YouTube was tiny in comparison to what it is worth now," says Hennessey. Still, many high-tech acquisitions don't work out in the end. What has Google learned about how to manage them? In Hennessey's experience, "a lot of acquisitions fail because nobody asked the hard questions they should have asked at the beginning." In his view, the justification for a partnership or acquisition should be tested as brutally as is possible. The echo chambers we've discussed can prevent this from happening: "Normally these acquisitions of public companies are done by a small team and the number of people that even know about is tiny. So, you really have to make sure that the story holds water if you bring it out to thousands of employees."*

Few other companies embody this potential for innovation through a recombination of already available ideas and capabilities like Dyson. The company's Airblade product line is almost a textbook case of taking a core capability from one area—cyclone technology from their vacuum product line—and creatively putting it to use in a completely different segment to produce one of the most effective and successful hand dryers in the market. Naturally, successes such as these are no accident, and the company has a pioneering approach to nurturing the internal collaborations necessary for such creative output. Social learning has been at the core of the company from the start.

The story of Dyson's success begins with James Dyson being frustrated about how poorly his vacuum cleaned the carpet. "What attracted me [to vacuum cleaners] was that they were an unloved object. Manufacturers made them. They didn't really care what they were making. They were just copying each other. It had become a commodity. I got really excited about that." Starting as a one-man show, Dyson was inspired by the way industrial sawmills clean the air with centrifugal separators. After 5127 prototypes, he developed the first bagless vacuum cleaner based on a "cyclone" technology. Trusting in social learning, Dyson built on ideas from others, imitated them, and finally made the unconventional connection to transfer one technology to other products.

Yet while it was the launch pad for Dyson's business, this technological advancement alone did not define Dyson's success. Instead, Dyson continuously rewrites engineering rules by creating an unbreakable bond between revolutionary cyclone technology and unexpected design. In traditional product-development processes, development and design are two separate functions in sequential order. At Dyson, commercial hand dryers, bladeless residential fans, hairdryers, and more all have two things in common: their designs had remained unchanged for decades and are now being revolutionized by the force of new connections.

James Dyson understood from the start the opportunity that lay in breaking silos and establishing a nourishing environment for boundary-spanning collaborations. But how does a company achieve borderless organizational nervous systems? Instead of separating specialist areas, Dyson created teams of "design engineers" who attended equally to design and engineering functions in the whole process, from product concept planning to final testing. Think of the unique shape of the Dyson Supersonic hairdryer, with its hole in the middle. During the development process, this shape proved essential to the machine's function but called for a new heating element. The team was able to combine expertise from design, electrical, and test engineering to achieve this.

Through many design decisions, Dyson creates an environment that connects functionalities and bridges knowledge barriers. In addition to Research, Design, and Development (RDD) teams, Dyson established several mechanisms for freeing idea flow. For instance, Dyson creates space for employees to acquire tacit knowledge outside of their functionality, embracing face-to-face exchange. One concrete way that the organization manages to create such an environment is the layout of its offices. Aiming to establish a sense of unity, Dyson places its design engineers at the center of each floor. There are no partitions or walls between the individual departments, making it impossible at first to tell who belongs to which department.

James Dyson said about his approach: "You are just as likely to solve a problem by being unconventional and determined as by being brilliant." As the continued innovative output of his company shows, sometimes all it takes to achieve this is designing systems that consistently put the right people together in a room.

On top of the direct effect of creating a set-up that fosters the identification of creative opportunities, such measures also have the indirect effect of enabling new cross-functional collaboration lines throughout the organization. Through the experience of collaborating, team members have the potential to develop into broker roles and nudge the organization's collaborative signatures toward a more connected idea flow. We will return to a more detailed discussion of this effect later in the book.

Up to now, we have mostly discussed ways of connecting diverse perspectives within an organization. The creative tension between these perspectives is important for discovering innovative opportunities—but since these are often located among different tribes, leaders often have to actively manage collaborations to nurture these types of collisions. Research shows that new ventures with board members with diverse backgrounds in a range of industries out-innovate start-ups with more homogeneous board members. The diverse (social) learnings a leader brings to the table helps them and their teams to spot innovative potential.

> **Quick Win:**
> - Build a platform for internal exchange to foster idea creation across the entire organization. It can be a simple SharePoint that gives employees the chance to share their ideas.
> - Store innovation leads in a location that is accessible to all employees—to read *and* edit—either virtually or locally in your office.
> - Set up a program in which any employee can put an idea forward with the possibility of getting funding, a time budget, and the help of innovation experts.
> - Engage in face-to-face exchange and create events for sharing experiences and ideas—for example, regular cross-department breakfasts for knowledge exchange.
> - Think about recombining already available ideas and capabilities; don't shy away from building on ideas from others, transferring them to your area of operations.
> - Break silos, bridge knowledge barriers, and establish a nourishing environment for boundary-spanning collaborations—across departments and divisions.
> - Create space for employees to acquire tacit knowledge outside of their functionality, and embrace face-to-face exchange, for example through office design.
> - Actively manage cross-organizational collaboration. For example, offer rewards for all ideas/projects that evolve between different teams/departments.
> - Find board members from a diverse range of industries.

> *Leader's Voice: Transforming a traditional R&D unit into a company builder*
> *"Invention is about burning money, innovation is about making money." When Thorsten Mueller took over as Osram's chief technology officer, the company was at the precipice of a major transformation. A longstanding leader in the illuminant industry, Osram's legacy business model was being disrupted by technological advances: LED technology had increased the average lifespan of a light bulb from a couple thousand hours to up to one hundred thousand. No longer*

could you treat lightbulbs as consumables and base revenue streams on their burning out regularly and being replaced.

The company had two options: a last-man-standing strategy, which would cash out on the illuminant products as long as they were still generating revenues, a new business model based on core capabilities. Management was decisively in favor of the latter option, with no looking back. The company decided to sell its legacy illuminant business in 2015/2016. Either it would succeed in changing its positioning from consumables manufacturer to high-tech firm or it would be left without any market niche at all.

Over the following years, Osram developed new business models around the intersection of optical semi-conductors and digital technologies: sensing solutions (such as optimized facility usage), treatment solutions (such as urban farming), and display solutions. Crucial for this success was a fundamental shift within the R&D unit. Traditionally, R&D had been responsible for purely technical, rather incremental product innovation the company's core business Now innovation had to be on the level of the business model, focusing on solutions rather than commodity products.

This was a tall order, especially given the time schedule: "The expectation was to present a roadmap for our new strategy just 20 days after I started my new job," Mueller recalls. In order to achieve this, he had to completely re-design the company for collaborative advantage.

His first critical change focused on collaboration between R&D and the business units. Traditionally, most of R&D's financing came from the business units in the form of very small-scale contract research. This was changed to a guaranteed budget as a fixed percentage of turnover from each business unit. "I told the board, 'You will get angry calls from every business unit CEO, but we have to make this decision now and stand by it,' Mueller told us. "Even the BU CEOs had to chuckle when confronted with the fact they were funding over 300 mini R&D projects. The new structure completely changed the conversation: Rather than a lot of very incremental projects, we were doing only a couple of strategically crucial projects with real firepower behind them." The R&D unit got financial stability, and the business units got more say in defining the strategic initiatives the R&D unit were to explore.

For Mueller, this was part of a larger program to change the way R&D and the business units interacted. A core new function he established was that of program manager, a person who would coordinate the strategic initiatives, which were co-defined between business units and R&D in order to ensure real co-creation. The program managers were staffed cross-functionally: some had R&D backgrounds, some had BU backgrounds, and some came from outside the company, bringing with them fresh perspectives.

All of this amounted to much greater and much more strategic collaboration between business and R&D was the core of Mueller's agenda: "Just on

> *a language level, it was extremely important to be able to translate between the language of the business who thinks in EBIT and RoIC and the language of the R&D engineers thinking about quantum effects,"* he says.
>
> The transformation to a more strategic role for R&D was further enhanced by greater strategic collaborations across the company. For example, Mueller established rotations between R&D engineers and BU managers. For all functions, he increased direct interactions with end-customers, including by setting up fieldtrips for the board.
>
> But it was not all about internal collaboration; external openness was increased. For example, the externalization of R&D projects went from below 10 percent to 40 percent, *"in order to challenge not-invented-here syndrome."* Strategic acquisitions, such as buying one of the fastest-growing start-ups for indoor cannabis farming in Europe, further developed capabilities and market positions in the strategic growth markets central to Osram's new focus on solutions.
>
> Finally, discipline was required—to kill unsuccessful initiatives: *"We evaluated our industry 4.0 project and discontinued it after six months although all of our peers were doing these kinds of projects. It was just not the best use of our resources."* Mueller recalls.
>
> Altogether, the changes were a wild success. *"I had people change from being scientists to becoming entrepreneurs. That was the most motivating thing,"* says Mueller. And through its new positioning, the company could achieve a much higher valuation—one more suitable to a high-tech company than a commodities manufacturer—when they later merged with AMS, an Austrian 3D sensing specialist.

4.2 Balance Internal and External Collaboration

We have discussed at length collaboration between departments, functions, and even social cliques. It is equally important to consider the collaboration signatures within these tribes of employees—the people who work in very similar functions and collaborate regularly as part of the job description. How do these individuals, who interact daily within the same teams, relate to one another? And how do these interactions affect their ability to sense innovative opportunities?

Answering these questions might seem straightforward: "war stories" from the start-up world, as well as from successful corporate turnarounds, emphasize the importance of strong, "cult-like" connections within the innovative venture. As we will see later in the book, our vision of a collaborative organization recognizes the many benefits of such strong internal connections and provides concrete guidance for how to create them. However, we also offer some cautionary notes. Indeed, many of the concepts discussed so far might seem to stand in direct contrast with this managerial intuition. Haven't we been warning against the sort of echo chambers dense networks can create? And isn't there a tradeoff between internal collaboration and the ability to reach and get perspectives from more diverse and distributed tribes?

Consider the case of an innovation project at a multinational automotive company that will remain nameless. At its various production sites, the company tasked cross-functional teams with coming up with innovations for how new products would be developed. Amid this process, an analysis of the Indian subsidiary revealed that the team with the lowest internal collaboration intensity was vastly more innovative than other teams. In five years, it had generated almost *twice as many innovations* as all the other teams at the same site combined.

How to explain this? Working well with other people usually means learning from them and being inspired by their ideas; but at the same time, it also often involves sharing biases—theirs with you, yours with them. People who engage with each other frequently, and with intensity, especially in collaborative work, tend to form shared mental models. These are good for collaboration to the extent that they allow for alignment and coordination. However, they can be bad for the generation of creative ideas, especially ideas that break the shared mental model's fundamental logic.

How can managers navigate this conundrum? Here is the short version. A strong focus on internal collaboration engenders vast amounts of energy within a tribe of employees such as a department, a project team, or a local office. This collaborative energy can drive productivity as well as incremental learning. Through intense interactions, both tricks-of-the-trade and best practices flow effortlessly through the tribe. A strong sense of belonging and shared identity drive members to go above and beyond for their peers. At the same time, the tribe often pays a price for this: A strong sense of belonging can develop into an unwillingness to consider anything that is perceived as "foreign"; shared best practices cannot be questioned. In other words, by focusing on what is shared and similar within the tribe, everything that is different is driven out of the shared cognitive system. Predictably, this can be detrimental to the ability of the group to self-correct and, thus, to innovate. Conversely, the less connected team in the Indian subsidiary was not held back by these factors. They were able to bring their diverse expertise to exploring creative opportunities, disagreeing constructively, and experiencing creative tensions. In this environment, innovation blossomed.

How to recreate that Indian team's successes in your company? If you ever find that all the ideas generated in your team are feeling too similar, take a step back and try another approach.

> **Quick Win:**
> 1. Randomly select seven people from your company and bring them together.
> 2. Explain the problem you have right now, without giving any hint of solutions your team has already discussed, and let them use their experience and expertise to brainstorm possible directions.
> 3. Encourage them to be bold and to think outside the box. Make the ground rules clear from the start. These might include the promise that no idea will be judged, or that wild ideas are encouraged, one conversation at a time, and if possible, always draw your idea instead of only writing words on the post-it.
>
> The right brainstorming warm-up can move people into a more creative mindset. Ask your group one of the two questions:
> "How might a legless chicken cross the road?" or "How can we generate a convertible feeling within a closed car?" Let them brainstorm answers for two minutes before coming to your real problem.

To further illustrate the effects of within-tribe collaborative signatures, let's consider two extreme examples. First, imagine a group with a low expression of internal collaboration focus. This could be a group that just recently formed and contains no strong existing ties. As such, new norms and new ideas can be established fairly quickly, since no momentum and rigidity is counteracting them. There is no established culture or "way to do things here," which often makes transformation efforts so hard in many organizations.

On the other end of the extreme, consider a group with very high internal collaboration focus. A good example would be a family, with its tight-knit of social relations and closely coordinated social interaction patterns. Here, it is tough to affect change to established routines. Once dysfunctional patterns are established, they can be incredibly hard to interrupt, requiring years of work—even if every family member agrees that the interaction patterns don't serve the group's well-being. In these situations, psychologists have to employ quite radical interventions just to disrupt the social patterns; only if this is achieved can new routines be learned.

In organizations, most groups fall somewhere between these extremes, with knock-on effects for productivity and adaptability.

> **Lesson Learned:**
> Be aware of the two-sided sword:
>
> - Strong internal collaboration within a team fosters energy, a sense of belonging and productivity.
> - However, it can also prevent diverse, outside ideas and collaborations with other teams from entering the frame, hindering innovative potential.
>
> As is often the case, the ideal lies somewhere in the middle: Close relationships create a familiar atmosphere and culture, but looser ties hinder rigidity and loosen ties.

4.3 Connect Networks of Innovators

Organizations have developed a variety of simple measures to disrupt the social momentum, reduce rigidity and open up spaces for innovation. A fairly well-known example with limited intrusion in the normal work processes is Adobe's approach to sourcing bottom-up innovation projects. The company's "Kickstart" program enables any employee with a vision to sign up for an innovation workshop, where he or she will receive a budget of $1000 to build a prototype and test the idea. Once selected for funding, the employee breaks free of his old social work environment and works full time on his vision. Often, we have observed companies starting such initiatives but then aborting them after a few years, disappointed with the results. Sadly, such initiatives are not "plug and play" but need to be deliberately managed and nurtured. As the chief technology officer at Bühler, one of the world's leading plant equipment manufacturers, told us: "In the first years, you won't get many transformative ideas. The skill needs to be built first. But what you do get is an address list of employees who are excited about innovation, who are willing to go above and beyond, who want to shape the future of the company. By connecting and empowering these people, you will build the innovativeness of your company long-term."

Another approach for increasing collaborative reach is fostering informal exchanges. An example might be what some call/we call lunch roulette. You pair employees who are not in regular contact, giving them the opportunity to discuss topics outside their own field. There are different ways to pair people. You could do a short availability survey and simply match individuals who are free at the same time, or you might randomly select people on the intranet and send out an invite. You could also ask employees to identify a part of the organization with which they have little contact, or about which they know little, and make connections from there.

At Daimler, you've got a twist on the idea: lunch & learn. In 30-minute keynote speeches, employees present their current projects, show and test together new methods and tools, or exchange ideas. This gives people a look outside their own bubble and invites feedback from peers with new perspectives and skillsets. It can lead to drastic improvement on a project, but it can also have a big impact on a company's atmosphere and mood. We have experienced that employees feel more connected to each other and to the company if they know each other's problems and are able to help.

Perhaps the easiest approach to increasing collaborative reach is to increase the contact your innovators have with people from outside the organization. IDEO, a design and product-development consultancy, is an undisputed leader in innovation. Founded by Design Thinking inventor Kelley, it boasts clients that include Apple, Coca-Cola, and Bank of America. One of their methods for spotting innovative opportunities is "unfocus groups." Rather than test ideas or products on typical users, as a focus group might, they go out of their way to find atypical users. For example, in designing a new shoe, they gathered the perspectives of (among others) a dominatrix and a foot-fetishist. Even if you feel your company is too conservative and specialized for this approach, we suggest that you might benefit from more early contact with outside perspectives in the "messy front-end" of innovation. For example, a traditionally rather conservative manufacturing company we have worked with invited start-ups from the sex toy market to co-create more sensually appealing product designs.

A final approach we have seen companies take is to be very deliberate in designing varying collaboration patterns for the different phases of innovation. Imagine having to take a sharp left while driving. What steps do you take? You slow down. This is normal: drivers are constantly adjusting their pace according to the task at hand. You drive swiftly when it's safe, and break when you need to, for example, just before turning, and then you accelerate again. There is a parallel strategy for managing the internal collaborative signature of your organization in order to support innovation. The key is differentiating between times when *creative opportunities need to be gathered* and when *productivity and execution of one of those ideas should be the focus*.

The most successful tribes oscillate between exploring perspectives from other tribes during idea generation and increasing the internal collaborative focus when it comes to execution. Creative productivity can be predicted in a variety of contexts just by looking at which teams show this pattern of oscillation. A more radical version of this approach is to physically remove a group tasked with coming up with innovative opportunities from the tribe of their peers in the daily business. For example, Nestle has acknowledged the need for their more exploratory businesses to have a different way of collaborating than their more exploitative core businesses [9]. This is why the Nespresso unit occupies its own, separate corner of the campus.

> **Quick Win:**
> How to reduce rigidity and open up space for innovation:
> - Create programs that enable any employee with a vision to sign up for an innovation workshop, which includes a budget to build a prototype and test the idea.
> - Foster informal exchanges through lunch roulette or lunch & learn to bring together employees who do not work with each other regularly.
> - Increase your innovators' contacts with people from outside your organization, especially those with unconventional perspectives. For example, send your creative geniuses to networking events, or set up an "Innovation Board" staffed with external experts.

Let's look further at how companies vary collaborative patterns. At Boeing, we can observe a concrete example of oscillating tribes. Members of a so-called "Phantom" workgroup join teams during different phases of the product innovation process. The Phantom team's internal collaboration is already intense, and distributing members elsewhere enables free communication flow between the teams. Moreover, by joining a team, the Phantom member disrupts established patterns and gets access to new ideas. At Pivotal, a tech firm, software is usually written in teams of two. During the development process, the pairs get to know each other well, establish routines, and collaborate intensely. But once the software development phase ends, the pairs split, and the members are re-paired with a new teammate for the next project.

The Valve corporation is a true pioneer in nurturing internal collaborations; it is also one of the most innovative and successful players in its industry [10]. As a premier video game publisher, the studio rose to international acclaim with their Half-Life and Counter-Strike brands. But even from its inception, the company set itself apart through its leadership approach—or to be exact, by not having predefined leaders at all. What the co-founders, Gabe Newell and Mike Harrington, former Microsoft employees and passionate gamers, wanted to build was a company that avoids internal fault lines and barriers between developer and consumer. They viewed the approaches of their former employers as wrong-headed, and believed that even innovative companies fell short in unleashing creative potential.

To be more precise, let's look at the spark-moment of frustration and confusion most often cited by Gabe Newell. Newell noticed that a competitor with a twelve-person team outperformed Microsoft. Through direct distribution, the small company talked directly to customers rather than getting feedback on their products from retailers. Gabe and Mike also needed to find a new way to collaborate in order to realize their vision—to do everything differently compared to the silicon valley's pitfalls back then they needed to nurture their collaborative advantage.

> **Deep Dive: Collaborative Innovation at Valve**
> The most illustrative artifact of the collaborative advantage the founders wanted to develop in their company is also one of the first touchpoints new employees have with the company. If you start at Valve, you'll receive a handbook with 56 pages that explain everything from facts about Valve and its corporate culture, how remuneration works, the specific role of the employee, and how projects are chosen, and a glossary with the most important phrases. The booklet also features a section on what Valve is bad at—a degree of self-reflection many companies would find uncomfortable. Everyone receives the same booklet. This might seem strange, given the range of roles they must hire for. But within Valve there are no positions assigned to employees, no team leaders or managers. That's also one of the first things that new employees read in the handbook: "*We want innovators, and that means maintaining an environment where they'll flourish. That's why Valve is flat. It's our shorthand way of saying that we don't have any management, and nobody 'reports to' anybody else. We do have a founder/president, but even he isn't your manager. This company is yours to steer—toward opportunities and away from risks. You have the power to green-light projects. You have the power to ship products.*"
>
> What is the thinking behind this? As Gabe explains, "People who are constantly looking for the opportunity to do something new are also people who are not going to be helped by having job titles. Job titles create expectations of specialization and focus which don't map really well to creating the best possible experience for your customers."
>
> Key to making this lofty aspiration work in practice are two organizational practices: Polyarchy and social proofs. Despite the colorful names, these are not rules taken from an artist commune, but concrete practices that anchor and guide how employees at Valve work together and how the organization makes important decisions.
>
> Polyarchy essentially means that decision-making authority is delegated to individuals with the richest information, the most relevant expertise, and the

most immediate incentives. Valve believes that self-selection yields more reliable and lower-cost information and therefore faster market responsiveness than traditional controls and incentives. In other words, the person with the most information should be the one who decides. What kind of decisions fall under this dictum? The answer is: every single one. From which project to work on to who to recruit for the project team; from establishing budgets and setting timelines to who the track progress; and so on. A good example of that is their product platform called Steam but more about that later.

While polyarchy ensures rapid decision-making and avoids internal bottlenecks, it leaves a substantial issue of alignment. After all, if all decision-making is decentralized, how are synergies across the organization realized? How can strategic direction be established and path dependencies with other departments considered? The answer lies in Valve's second practice, which balances the speed and innovativeness of polyarchy with a selection and alignment mechanism. The clue: Even this mechanism, the purview of middle management in more traditional organizations, is relational rather than formal.

Valve uses social proofs, as well as peer evaluation-based remuneration and performance-review systems, as counterbalances to polyarchy. Peer reviews were started as a way for employees to give one another useful feedback on how to best grow as individual contributors. As for compensation, Valve says its goal is a "correct" figure: "We tend to be very flexible when new employees are joining the company, listening to their salary requirements and doing what we can for them," reads the starter pack. "Over time, compensation gets adjusted to fit an employee's internal peer-driven valuation. That's what we mean by 'correct'—paying someone what they're worth (as best we can tell using the opinions of peers)." People are asked to rate their colleagues based on four metrics:

1. **Skill Level / Technical Ability**: How difficult and valuable are the kinds of problems you solve? How important/critical of a problem can you be given? Are you uniquely capable (in the company? industry?) of solving a certain class of problem, delivering a certain type of art asset, contributing to design, writing, music, etc.?
2. **Productivity/Output**: How much shippable (not necessarily shipped to outside customers), valuable, finished work did you get done?
3. **Group Contribution**: How much do you contribute to studio process, hiring, integrating people into the team, improving workflow, amplifying your colleagues, or writing tools used by others?
4. **Product Contribution**: How much do you contribute at a larger scope than your core skill? How much of your work matters to the product? How much did you influence correct prioritization of work or resource

trade-offs by others? Are you good at predicting how customers are going to react to decisions we're making?

Through this evaluation process, employees are nudged toward contributing as much as possible to the company and also toward selecting wisely the project they are working on, since remuneration is directly linked to performance.

It's that balance we've been talking about—between acting independently by making decisions without multiple rounds of meetings and consultation and yet caring about colleagues' rating your work, since this will ultimately determine your pay.

So, how do you select the project you are working on as an employee? Valves advises: "You were hired to constantly be looking around for the most valuable work you could be doing. [...] here's no rule book for choosing a project or task at Valve. But it's useful to answer questions like these:

- Of all the projects currently under way, what's the most valuable thing I can be working on?
- Which project will have the highest direct impact on our customers? How much will the work I ship benefit them?
- Is Valve not doing something that it should be doing?
- What's interesting? What's rewarding? What leverages my individual strengths the most?"

What's even more interesting about Valve is how they work together. Valve functions in the logic of individual "cabals." A cabal is a multidisciplinary project team that is self-organized and temporary. The most suitable person in the cabal emerges as the team leader: "The leaders serve the team, while acting as centers for the teams." Leaders change from one project to the next. During a project, teams work extremely close together and establish their own way of thinking and operating. As employees decide which teams to join, they are encouraged to ask others what they are working on, and to challenge others' ideas about what is working and what isn't. As such, all employees are highly aware of what is going on throughout the company, and connecting with other people. Valve wants collisions within its talent pool; these, it believes, are crucial to the success of the company.

You might argue that this can go quickly off course. And you'd be right. In Gabe's words: "Where that bites you is if somebody makes a bad decision, like Diretide. I found out that we were doing something stupid when one of our customers mailed me and said 'you're doing something stupid.' I was like 'really?' And I go and find out that yes, in fact, we're doing something stupid. That isn't a fault, it's just one of those trade-offs." Gabe's mindset is that the most important thing at Valve is that they are constantly learning from one another, constantly challenging their status quo, and that the best-informed person takes the decisions.

Valve also has three pages of that welcome handbook dedicated to failure, showing that making a mistake is not grounds for termination: "Screwing up is a great way to find out that your assumptions were wrong or that your model of the world was a little bit off. As long as you update your model and move forward with a better picture, you're doing it right. Look for ways to test your beliefs. Never be afraid to run an experiment or to collect more data."

How did this unique approach enabled Valve to become one of the most innovative and successful players (if you excuse the pun) in the video game industry? Let's take a look at how their crown jewel, the video game platform Steam, was developed in order to find out. Valve needed a platform on which they could easily update their multiplayer games. Since there was nothing like this on the market at the time, a team of innovative employees organically pooled their resources to create it themselves. They mapped the idea onto a potential market opportunity. They convinced others with their idea and to join the project, floated their ideas with potential users, and launched the platform, called Steam, in September 2003. Today, Steam has grown to become a digital distribution platform for video games. In fact, it is *the* digital distribution platform, not only for games developed by Valve but for almost every game from every studio. It turned Valve from game developer to game developer, publisher, and game distributor. With over 120 million monthly active users and 62.6 million daily active players in 2020, it is the most popular platform of the gaming industry. Seventy-five percent of all games downloaded globally onto PCs are sold through Stream. And all this happened because a group of employees saw the need for a distribution platform and were able to work toward that goal, and see how it developed, without any bureaucratic obstacles. This project did not come from a top-down process such as analysis of the competition, formal market research, or the need for a new project to fit a budgeting cycle. Through the polyarchic approach, Valve delivers steady improvements in consumer engagement, project team motivation, and speed to market.

But as you might be starting to note, Valve is not the sort of company to stop there. It went a step further with Steam. Noting that customers wanted to modify games themselves, the company decided to forge a unique relationship with their customers.

As Valve employee Robin Walker describes it, years ago in a forum thread, two users started creating graphics for hats in the game Team Fortress 2. Valve took note and created a place for user-submitted content. This turned into Steam Workshop, a massive marketplace where users share or sell game tweaks. "The interesting thing is that it didn't start with us having some grand vision

> of the future around user-generated content," Walker says. "It started with customers doing something interesting and other customers clearly saying, 'I like that, and I want it.' And us going: 'How do we scale that? How do we get to the point where everyone can do that?'" These customer modifications to games are called "mods," and Valve's willingness to let users create, share, and even sell them sets Steam apart. The company not only increased collaboration with customers, but it also created value-capture opportunities for both those customers and the company. Today there are mods for almost every game available. Consider Skyrim, from publisher Bethesda, which raked in game-of-the-year awards and is considered by many one of the best video games of all time. In its first week on the market, Skyrim sold more than seven million copies, generating an estimated revenue of $450 million. The Steam Workshop lists over 28,000 mods for Skyrim, which have extended the game's appeal and marketability, and those of its follow-up games, well past the normal lifespan of a video game. The mods also unlock new revenue streams: For every mod sold, the developer receives a quarter of the sales; Valve, as platform owner, and the related game's publisher share the remaining 75 percent between them.

4.4 Three Take-Aways for Leaders

Let's return briefly to eToro. As you'll recall, technical nudges that changed the trading network's collaboration signatures doubled profitability. But this was a research exercise: the changes were discontinued after some time and the original context re-established. How did the traders respond? In a nutshell, they reverted to their old interaction patterns and formed the same echo chambers that served them so poorly in the first place. The profitability of the trading network returned to its baseline level.

Why didn't the traders, who had experienced the performance benefits of interacting in a new way, want to keep doing what worked so well?

To understand this behavior, you need to understand two principles that are essential to managing for collaborative advantage. First, while people often intuitively accept many of the central ideas behind collaborative advantage, the actual collaboration signatures governing their own behavior and performance are mostly invisible to them. If we were to ask managers whether exchanges and communication are important for innovation, most would say they are. However, when we ask people to describe the collaboration signatures in their own organizations, their intuitive assessments are mostly guesswork, and only loosely related to what we find when we later analyze the organization.

There are many reasons we are unable to intuitively grasp the collaborative architecture that surrounds us. Some are emotional—that is, our desire to view our social relationships in a way that benefits our sense of self-worth—and some are to do with perception, or lack thereof: many important interactions occur without our observing them. The most likely explanation for why the traders returned to their old interaction patterns is that they simply didn't see what had changed. For them, it was just an unusually good trading season; the reason behind their fortunes was wholly inaccessible to them.

This leads to the second important principle. Since most people don't have intuitive access to their collaboration signatures, you can't count on their intuitive learning to create the most adaptive and functional interaction patterns. If you want to fully capitalize on the potential of collaborative advantage in your organization, you have to actively manage it.

This has been a lot of information. Let's look at three central take-aways:

From i-nnovation to we-nnovation: Capitalize on social learning

While we like to credit individuals for great innovations, the biggest steps forward are the product of smartly managed collaborations. Optimal learning strategies focus 90 percent of effort on social learning and only 10 percent on individual learning in complex environments.

> **Lesson Learned:**
> If you want your employees to learn a new skill or develop a new mindset, one of the easiest solutions is often to build engaging and sustained interfaces between them and role models who already excel at your new learning goal.

> **Quick Win:**
> Foster strategic mentorships between employees of different skills, experiences and positions in the corporate hierarchy.

From consensus to collisions: Overcome silos

Great innovations depend on the right exchanges rather than the most exchanges. In particular, collisions between diverse perspectives are the fuel of surprising ideas. For example, we have seen in the case of the international asset manager that collaborative reach into otherwise separated silos was a necessary condition for unusual innovativeness.

> **Lesson Learned:**
> Beware the echo chamber and design collaborations to counteract the blinding effects of social conformity pressures and confirmation biases.

> **Quick Win:**
> Before bringing an idea to action, validate it across different teams in your organization that are operating in completely different areas.

From size to reach: Innovate in ecosystems

Managers who acknowledge the importance of informal collaborations for innovation often simply try to maximize those. This can introduce huge collaborative cost while still failing to increase innovative output.

> **Lesson Learned:**
> If you want to help your employees become more innovative, build them bridges to new groups such as through direct customer interfaces or easy access to a strong external partner network rather than with new people from the same groups.

> **Quick Win:**
> Establish regular think tanks with your employees and your customers and/or external business partners to foster external knowledge exchanges.

4.5 Ideas for Action: Simple Practices

In order to get you started, here are some easy-to-implement practices that organizations have adopted to nurture more innovative collaborations.

Relational Onboarding. When onboarding new hires, think beyond integrating them into their core team and getting their laptops set up. Take inspiration from Gore and have a list of key contacts from throughout the company whom new hires need to get to know in the first two months. Have a mentor make introductions.

Internal Fellowships. Bottlenecks in the collaboration flow often take place laterally, between separate units. Take inspiration from SAP and implement a program of internal fellowships. One design idea: Notify employees of specific challenges in particular business units and give them a three-month window in which to apply to tackle them. If someone from a different unit is brought on to work on the challenge, his salary will come from the receiving unit and from a central fund. The unit he's being borrowed from will be one man down—but leaders there will get credit for having encouraged their team members to help out across the company.

Reverse Mentors. Other typical issues relate to bottom-up information flows. Encourage your middle managers to take on "reverse mentors": younger employees on the forefront of relevant technologies or in direct operational contact with customers.

Zero barriers. Interfaces between employees and either customers or external partners are points where idea flow often breaks down. Set up field trips for developers. It is important to bring empathy deep into organizations. Consider the example of Stripe. Set explicit goals for managers about how often they should visit customers in person. Track direct customer interactions as KPIs.

4.6 Ideas for Action: Advanced Practices

If you want to go a step further to increase collaborative innovation, here are some ideas for how.

Idea Meritocracy. Take a page out of Bridgewater's playbook and establish an idea of meritocracy: An internal environment where the best ideas win. Make expertise visible (Bridgewater uses "baseball cards" for each employee, with areas of expertise listed). This helps you include the right people and find scalable ways to access and aggregate their ideas as management inputs (think Dot Collector). Finally, monitor the quality of the decision and continuously evolve and fine-tune your process.

Break up rigid structures. Take inspiration from Samsung and expose sheltered internal suppliers and service organizations more directly to market inputs and pressures. Practices such as dual sourcing (that is, setting up equal playing fields and giving units the freedom to source externally) and parallel development for strategically important projects break path dependencies and unlock real options.

Decentralize decision-making. Follow Valve's approach and let your employees take a more active role in deciding where their capabilities should be deployed. This should be combined with clear coordination mechanisms and local incentive systems to avoid diffusion of responsibility.

4.7 Collaborative Innovation in Action: LEGO

By now, we have learned a lot about collaborative advantage, its (sometimes counterintuitive) mechanisms, and best practice approaches to nurture it for innovation. While we have seen strategies for mastering either internal or external collaborations, we want to end here by focusing on a company that did both.

Multi-colored plastic bricks offer endless opportunities to bring ideas to life; few toy manufacturers have done as much as LEGO to fuel future generations' imaginations. It seems hard to imagine today that the iconic Danish brand once was on the brink of shutting down.

In the late 1990s, LEGO faced dwindling profits in a competitive market. With production in Denmark, the company's executives had limited room to compete on pricing with giants such as Walmart and ToysRUs profiting from cheap production overseas. LEGO was going to have to change course. Eager to strengthen sales and develop the brand as a toy pioneer, rather than get into a cost-cutting race to the bottom, LEGO focused on innovation.

Lego had always been strong on creativity. However, with the senior management now leaning heavily on innovation to differentiate its products and defend profitability, that creativity went off on multiple tangents. From big hits such as LEGO Star Wars and LEGO Harry Potter to less successful projects like children's clothing, books, movies, and TV shows, LEGO lost focus and control. With increasing complexity in each and every part of the business, LEGO increased its costs, and the risks it was taking on, becoming even more vulnerable in a competitive market. It started the new millennium with a loss of DKK 831, and admitted in its annual report "we lost focus."

More specifically, the company relied heavily on separately operating business units without free information flow and knowledge exchange. The development team's mission was to come up with cool and exciting toys. At the same time, departments focusing on business goals tried to cope with the increasing complexity caused by the enormous product line extension. Without any connection to the core business, the designers came up with toys far from LEGO's original heritage, leading to overextension and dilution. LEGO had to learn the hard way the harm teams working in silos can do to overall performance. Instead of profiting from the boosted innovation, LEGO faced catastrophic business developments.

How did it manage to land on its feet, growing to become the world's largest toy manufacturer by revenues just a few years later? They stopped innovating outside the box and started innovating inside the brick. In other words, they realized development without strong interdependencies to business leads to distraction and chaos. They realized their need for interconnectedness and effective collaborative advantage.

With the initiative "Design for Business" (D4B), collaboration between the previously isolated creative and administrative teams became a key focus of future innovation projects. In this new design process, knowledge from across the company came together and blended into truly flourishing innovation. Instead of granting authority to the individual product innovation teams to decide which innovation would be pursued in the future, LEGO today relies on a Markets & Product division. This cooperation across all product and market-related teams is home to regional Concept Labs, units in charge of detecting local trends and advising the division management with the final decision-making competencies.

D4B led to one of the most significant successes in LEGO's history: LEGO Friends, targeting girls. Building on extensive market research, business experts set requirements for addressing young girls, which gave guidance to developing a whole new product line of construction play, including sets to build beauty salons, veterinary offices, and karate studios. Within just one year, the healthy interdependence of several departments tripled sales to girls.

In 2001, the fundamental changes first had borne fruit and led to a result improvement of DKK 1.6 bn despite restructuring costs of DKK 122 m. Besides realizing the importance of a strong relationship between development and its core business, LEGO made customers the focus of innovation. After refocusing internal innovation and embracing internal collaboration, LEGO prepared for external input from its stakeholder and initiated a pioneering culture of open innovation. Always aiming to create new interfaces with its customers, LEGO leveraged its brand value and its loyal fans as a source for new ideas. In the early days, LEGO started to co-create unique products with its stakeholders by bringing consumers into the initial stages of the product-development process. Nowadays, making use of technological advances, LEGO has created an innovation community across the globe. Using their millions of active users, they have established engagement platforms and forums where everyone can pitch their new toy ideas for crowd voting. After being approved by a LEGO review board and collecting 10,000 votes from the community, the vision turns into reality. The community was a win–win for all stakeholders: LEGO increases its innovative product portfolio, engagement, brand affinity, and external collaborations, creating new revenue sources. Users get access to a new platform to express their creativity and receive 1 percent of the sales of the design they proposed. In the past five years, LEGO Ideas lead to the development of 23 new innovative sets; almost all sold out in their first release.

> **Lesson Learned:**
> What can we learn from LEGOs past 20 years?
> Being aware and using methods to embrace interconnectedness and collaborative advantage has the power not only to transform one's business but also to bring together a whole organization and its stakeholders. Collaborative advantage, innovation, embracing exchange, breaking silos, leaning on interconnectedness, and bringing in external views are not simply a sequence of buzzwords, but necessary for success.

4.8 The Next Step

If you want to turbocharge collaborative innovation for your organization, go to collaborative-advantage.org/innovation for suggestions and resources on how to get started. Among others, you will find:

- A one-hour sample workshop to discuss the potential of collaborative innovation and potential action items with your relevant stakeholders (complete with agenda, pre-reads, suggested slides, and outcomes)
- A video of one senior leader's personal reflections on collaborative innovation.

You can also scan the QR Code. The resources are completely free.

References

In order to keep the book lean enough to comfortably be read on a plane, we have listed the full references on the companion website for your convenience. If you want to dig deeper, please check them out here:

8. Collaborative-advantage.org/references-innovation/8.
9. Collaborative-advantage.org/references-innovation/9.
10. Collaborative-advantage.org/references-innovation/10.

Part III

Collaborative Scaling

5

Hyperscaling Through Collaborations

> *The true mark of a leader is the willingness to stick with a bold course of action even as the rest of the world wonders why you are not marching in step with the status quo.*
> —Bill Taylor

5.1 Leverage Your Ecosystem to Scale Up Faster

"We are builders of companies, we are not innovators." Oliver Samwer, founder and chief executive of Rocket Internet doesn't want controversy. Yet when he and his fellow "despicable thieves," as the Silicon Valley press dubbed them, rang the bell of the Frankfurt Stock Exchange at 9.30 a.m. on October 2, 2014, they had every reason to be proud. Their initial public offering was oversubscribed ten times at the top end of the prize range and raised more than double the expected proceeds when the IPO was announced. And why shouldn't Rocket Internet become Europe's largest tech IPO in history at the time?! Investors were clearly excited about a company that had, since 2007, transformed from a modest start-up into one of Europe's largest technology companies, the parent of one in every four European start-ups with a valuation over $1 billion (a "unicorn" in Silicon Valley parlance).

The controversy centered on Rocket Internet's business model: copying, pretty much like-for-like, the strategies of successful (mostly Silicon Valley-based) start-ups, simply in untapped markets. These clones would be scaled up at incredible speed to achieve market-leading positions and then either sold to the company they were copying in the first place (effectively selling market access and established business infrastructure, and giving them a chance to envelop their leading competitor) or, if the company didn't want to cough up the cash, floating on the stock market, thus de-risking Rocket's portfolio position.

How could this model be successful? It all hinged on one core capability. In the words of Samwer, "We just build faster and better in more instances than anyone else." You don't need to be the first to have the idea if you out-execute everyone else. Rocket's ability to achieve incredible speed of growth and execution allowed the company to start from a follower position and still achieve market-leading dominance. Managers looking to drive this kind of speed and scale could do worse than look to Rocket as a model. How, then, did Samwer do it?

Start with their personal journeys and the learnings they derived from them. Samwer and his brothers spent brief stints as interns at various Silicon Valley start-ups before, in 1999, stumbling upon eBay. They (like many people) were excited by the potential of a digital auction house. Unlike others, though, they approached eBay's senior management and pitched them a plan to transfer the business model to Germany. Management was not ready to enter a new market—and in any case was not about to hand over implementation, if they did, to three interns. Unimpressed, the Samwers returned to Germany and set up an eBay clone called Alando. Their childhood toys were the first auctioned items. Over the next three months, through a relentlessly fast execution, the Samwers were able to outpace its fourteen competitors in customer growth, making Alando the biggest online auction house in Germany. A year later, eBay acquired Alando for $53 million, making the Samwer brothers the first internet millionaires in Germany—and deeply imprinting them with the experience's lessons. Chief among these was the importance of swift growth, and that it was possible to go from being laughed out of the room to receiving multiple millions in cash from the same people 12 months later. Over the coming years, the brothers would repeat and refine their model with a series of ventures, most notably a provider of ringtones called Jamba (sold to Verisign for $273 million in 2004).

In 2007, the brothers decided to structure and scale their model into a formal organization. Having learned the importance of speed, they decided to call the company Rocket Internet.

Rocket Internet formalized many of the principles with which the Samwers were already operating: the team systemically scanned business model innovations emerging from hubs such as Silicon Valley, with a shortlist kept of venture building opportunities. These opportunities would then be quickly vetted and, if deemed worth pursuing, rolled out in three to six emerging markets simultaneously. The degree of copying was often extensive: One founder of one of Rocket's portfolio companies remembers weekly meetings where every UI change made by the company they were copying—down to the color of each button on the website—was briefed for the technical team. Due to the emerging markets focus, transactions were usually optimized for mobile phones. With those details taken care of, the company was then entirely focused on Samwer's motto: "Scale. Scale. Scale. And the rest will come."

Rocket Internet was not only able to produce proven winners ready for public markets, such as Zalando (initially a clone of online shoe retailer Zappos), but could also sell smaller opportunities quickly. Bigpoint (an online gaming community) sold for $70 million in 2008 and MyCityDeal (a discount deal clone of Groupon, sold for 126 million in 2010 after a mere five months in operation). These smaller deals provided regular cash infusions that funded the longer expansion phases of the bigger opportunities.

Which practices allowed Rocket Internet to execute this strategy with incredible energy and unparalleled speed? It was a two-pronged solution: Enabling core decisions and eliminating distractions.

> The art of leadership is saying no, not saying yes. It is very easy to say yes.—Tony Blair

One of the core learnings from Rocket Internet is that eliminating clutter does just as much for an operation's speed as energizing core decision-making. The company ruthlessly standardized everything that was not core to the challenge of scaling an organization. These were all distractions. This included using off-the-shelf legal entities and standard contracts, as well as proprietary IT infrastructure such as ERP systems and web-shops optimized for the needs of high-growth start-ups. Hiring was carried out centrally for all the portfolio companies, and Rocket maintained both a stock of employees who could be staffed flexibly on projects in different portfolio companies as well as an established pipeline of suitable founders who could take over management roles. Even the basic timelines of building a new venture were standardized. Taken together, all of this meant that almost no managerial cognitive bandwidth was expended on what the Samwer brothers considered hygiene factors; all resources were focused 100 percent on one problem and one problem only: faster revenue growth than any competitor thought possible.

> **Self-Reflection:**
>
> What portion of your time and energy do you put toward your business's number one priority? What would you do if you had to cut the time you invested in everything else by half; would you delegate, standardize, ignore, outsource…?

In addition, Rocket Internet designed sophisticated practices and systems to ensure that critical decisions that would go a long way toward determining customer growth were enabled and energized by all their organizational knowledge about venture building. From the company's inception, staff were grouped by functional area, even if working for different portfolio companies. In this way, new marketing hires for a freshly minted e-commerce start-up would mix and match with their more experienced colleagues from mature portfolio companies. Aside from providing simple avenues for learning best practices, this had important psychological effects: It not only showed employees what type of speed and growth was possible by bringing them into contact with people like them who had helped create that sort of growth, it also set high internal benchmarks, with employees measuring themselves against their most successful peers (since unsuccessful companies would be quickly divested).

Consider the example of Wimdu, an Airbnb clone, which only a few weeks after its founding boasted 400 employees and more than 12,000 registered apartments. What are the motivational effects of sharing the office with the colleagues who have achieved such an incredible growth rate?

This type of competitive, standard-setting interaction was further supported in many other ways, too. For example, the company pulled together through detailed rule books with best practices for online marketing, and group-wide wikis and mailing lists with mini cases and learnings from functional experts. Oliver Samwer personally facilitated feedback sessions about successful, and less successful, initiatives with portfolio teams from all over the world. The same logic of peer learning and inspiration also applied on the manager level: managers at the parent group served as senior experts for the portfolio companies. While they did not assume formal leadership roles, these experts transmitted learnings, guided important decisions, and helped in crucial tasks such as acquiring critical customers. One level higher, each portfolio company had one of the Samwer brothers driving execution speed from an investor perspective. Managing directors of the portfolio companies also had to assume senior roles in at least one other portfolio company. Taken together, these practices ensured not only smooth, relatively effortless transmission of the capabilities of the company as a whole to each new portfolio company, but also a climate of collegial internal coopetition where one venture would dare the others to improve their growth rates.

Finally, the Rocket recipe put a unique twist on personnel policy, again because of the focus on fast growth. Instead of recruiting the technology-oriented and creative types that start-ups typically went after, Rocket looked for people more akin to investment bankers or management consultants. The primary attributes for selection were aggressiveness, a global approach, detail-oriented execution, and a deeply data-driven mindset. Incentive schemes were different than what you might normally see in the start-up world: Rocket's performance management was detailed and data-driven, based on internal benchmarks set by prior portfolio companies. The company paid higher salaries but granted less equity than more traditional incubators. At the same time, the track record of Rocket ventures made the equity very attractive to new hires: Better to have a small part of a gigantic pie than a large part of a much smaller one. Aggressive vesting schedules, meanwhile, ensured that founders' incentives were aligned with Rocket Internet's interests.

> **Lessons Learned:**
> Speed of execution and scale-up is a key success factor in organizations. Leveraging these requires eliminating any sort of distraction through standardization of tasks that are not related to the challenge. Crucial decisions also need to be infused with the maximum knowledge available, which can only be achieved by fostering cross-organizational learning, cooperation, and exchange. Energy levels in the organization can be vastly increased by designing and bringing crucial employees into regular contact with successful role models who work in similar functions.

After 2015, Rocket Internet began to transition from company builder to something more like a venture capital fund. This led to internal collisions with financial partners who felt Rocket was increasingly more competitor than creator of investment opportunities, a trend that culminated in Rocket's public split with its biggest partner, the Swedish investment group Kinnevik. On account of the Samwers' notoriety in the media, Rocket's accounting methods, which were sometimes more creative than befit a publicly listed company, and a stingy dividend policy, conflicts with shareholders mounted. Even though Rocket continued to produce extremely successful high-growth ventures such as HelloFresh and DeliveryHero (both IPOed in 2017), investor sentiment and market valuation of the parent company deteriorated. The brothers bought out minority shareholders and decided to delist Rocket in 2020.

Despite these misadventures in the public markets, Rocket Internet still stands for a unique recipe that allowed it to scale new ventures faster and more predictably than classical start-up incubators could manage. Its unique operating model illustrates a collaborative way of scaling one hypergrowth venture after the other. Beyond just leveraging outside ideas in a (super-) fast-follower strategy, Rocket's success was built upon carefully orchestrated synergies, learnings, and energy between portfolio companies through a hub structure.

Rocket demonstrates the potential of a modern, collaborative approach to scaling high-growth businesses. Leaders in many large organizations adopt a fast-follower strategy to innovation and want to see initial traction behind a new technology or market opportunity before investing their resources and brand in a risky innovation. This can be a profitable strategy, but only when the organization is able to outpace the first-movers in growth markets by deploying a superior resource. Fortunately, collaborative approaches to scaling allow organizations to quickly leverage resources to drive growth at breakneck speeds.

Leaders such as Shopify, Atlassian, and Slack all have built their incredible growth on more than 2000 API integrations with other technology companies. Online marketplace Alibaba expanded geographically by developing local businesses into strategic regional partners. WhatsApp serviced 400 million active users each month with only 50 employees before their acquisition by Facebook—by relying on strategic partners and outsourcing to eliminate path dependencies and scale operational resources much more quickly than they could have in-house. However, collaborative scaling goes beyond mere strategic partnerships with other businesses; consider how the Chinese high-tech manufacturer Huawei developed a strategic presence in Geneva in order to co-create technological standards in line with their own capability base.

This collaborative approach to scaling innovative ventures replaces silos and closed off labs with an externally cross-company and internally cross-functional way of doing things. Rather than considering scaling the task of logistics or market communication departments, it is all about leveraging partner networks. It strives to scale like a snowball—by carrying along the entire ecosystem as it rolls.

> **Self-Reflection:**
> Take a minute to think about your collaborations cross-functionally within your organization but also externally with strategic partners. Do you leverage the

possibilities of outsourcing and partnering to rapidly scale by focusing your company on just a few core capabilities? Could you run a leaner, faster-growing organization by better leveraging your partner networks?

5.2 Leverage Collaborative Networks to Scale Organically

Venture capitalists love to start their presentations with a popular meme about the relationship between ideas and the execution of these ideas (Fig. 5.1).

While clearly tongue-in-cheek and usually followed by a pitch about how differentiated that particular VC fund is, and how intimately they support their ventures in executing vision and scaling their business, the basic point still stands: there is a difference between *what innovative opportunity you pursue* and *how well you do it*. The most creative strategy is worthless if your organization is not successful in scaling it up in the real world.

In the last two chapters we looked at organizations as idea-processing machines: How can managers use collaborative advantage to optimize their ability to sense innovative opportunities? But just sensing innovative opportunities is not enough. In this chapter, we are going to take a look at how collaboration signatures influence the ability of organizations to scale up these ideas—and how you as an executive can smartly manage this scaling for collaborative advantage.

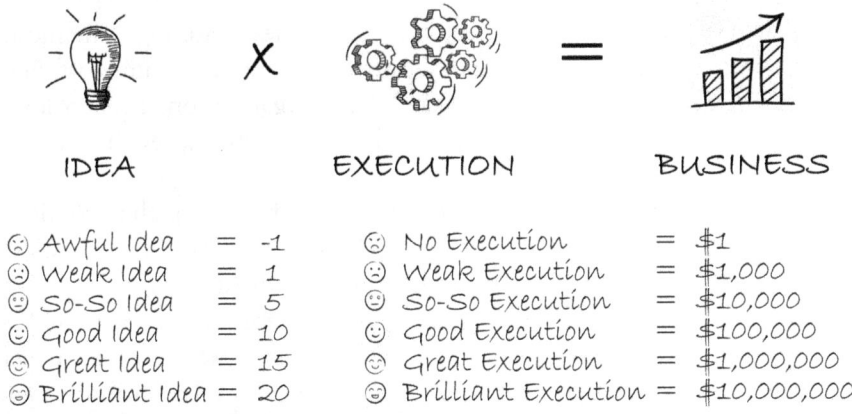

Fig. 5.1 Idea-execution link

Rocket Internet's unlikely success story already suggested some ways collaborative advantage can enable hypergrowth. Its internal hub structure allowed new ventures to leverage resources and knowledge from throughout the organization. This took the form of flexible staffing and rotations through shared managerial talent, standardized tools for non-core problems (such as scalable e-commerce platforms), and transfers of success recipes and inspiring results across the portfolio ventures. External resources were also embraced, chief among them through the sourcing of initial start-up ideas and product design from Silicon Valley companies.

But how might different organizations—ones that are not constantly building new companies—apply these principles? Let's find out by joining Tina (all names changed in this case), the incoming leader of a management consulting group's new strategy unit. She is aiming to scale her new unit by leveraging synergies across the organization [1].

> If we have data, let's look at data. If all we have are opinions, let's go with mine.—Jim Barksdale

Tina had inherited the unit from its high-flying former boss Tom, who had very quickly built it ground-up. The unit consisted of specialty sub-units such as joint-venture management and transformational change. In part because of his success with this project, Tom had now joined the company's executive ranks, and had personally tapped Tina to take over and scale his baby. The strategy unit had already grown quickly in its year and a half under Tom's leadership, but many opportunities remained for Tina to grasp. The biggest was the chance to improve collaboration with other units. As is typical for consulting companies, the organization was matrixed according to practices (Strategy, Talent, Supply Chain, etc.), industries (Banking, Chemicals, Natural Resources, etc.), and regions. In principle, the strategy unit's offerings could be put to good use in other parts of the organization through long-time full-service engagements. However, when Tina arrived, few industry or regional groups were calling on the unit.

To hit the ground running, and with the aim of scale up the promising unit quickly, Tina started with a collaboration analysis. This revealed quite a few surprising insights into how her new unit functioned.

First, many junior employees emerged as being absolutely central to the unit's operations—such as the administrative assistant who decided which team members would attend client engagement meetings. In addition, some very experienced, senior employees were fairly peripheral in the collaboration network, leaving their potential to drive revenue growth largely untapped.

Second, people were much less collaborative than Tina had hoped: Members of the unit were taking advantage of only 12 percent of the collaboration opportunities that were possible—compared with an optimal 30 percent. Consequently, employees were fairly disconnected: To get an answer to a question, they had to traverse, on average, three links of separation. For example, when Nicolas asks Tom to see a market segmentation of the unit performed for a client similar to the one, he is currently working for, Tom would send him to Ellie who had it, who in turn would forward Nicolas' request to Hanna, who could finally deliver the report. Many employees weren't willing (or simply didn't have the time) to go through this chain, which resulted in duplication of efforts and less-than-optimal outcomes for clients.

Based on these insights, Tina got to work unleashing growth with a laser focus rather than broadly encouraging "more collaboration." She centered her activities on two goals: improving collaboration effectiveness within her own unit and increasing the cross-selling potential with other parts of the organization.

First, she identified ten leaders who were central to the collaboration structure of her unit. She designated these respected individuals the "go to" experts for their specific fields, such as post-merger integration. This way, each content request was associated with a named representative who could proceed to distribute requests for collaboration throughout his or her network. In addition, leaders were asked to reach out to employees whom Tina's analysis had identified as being peripheral; they were to arrange one-to-one lunch dates with these individuals and ensure that they took part in client engagements.

Innovations from peripheral teams spread to the rest of the unit through creative methodologies. For example, one consultant had developed a new approach to managing communication about and within a transformation. Key ideas and outcomes were sent to important opinion leaders in the form of a postcard, together with an invitation to seek out the formerly hidden expert and discuss how his methods could apply to their projects.

In addition to these top-down interventions, Tina bet on the self-regulation of the employees. Each member of her unit was handed a visualization of their personal collaboration networks, together with relevant benchmarks and some tips on how to deploy their capabilities to greater effect. Data gleaned from Tina's initial collaboration analysis was also used lower down the hierarchy, to drive a data-driven, collaborative mindset. For example, after virtual meetings were analyzed, leaders called on quieter employees to share their perspectives—rather than waiting in vain for them to speak up.

An important measure of whether quick-scaling of a unit is going to be possible is the degree to which you see increases in efficiency. Tina assessed the time-saving impact of collaborating and seeking advice in her unit. She found that the 10 employees most often sought after for advice accounted for up to 50 percent of time savings through collaborations in the entire network. This identified overloaded experts who made many of their colleagues more effective but were not visible as formal leaders. Tina supported these experts through additional staff and resources, ensuring that they didn't burn out or become overwhelmed, stifling speed she needed for growing her business unit.

The analytics also revealed that about one in five collaborations deemed performance-critical were between individuals in her unit and people entirely outside the organization, from alumni to academics to professional associations. Tina tasked a well-connected leader with building an overview of these contacts and how to use them, and distributing this to the team, so that the connections could be deployed at scale rather than kept within the teams that had built the relationships.

Collaboration analytics also proved invaluable to her onboarding as a leader. For example, the post-merger integration subunit was the best performing in the wider strategy unit and had close ties with the former boss, Tom. Tom, who had background in PMI, had formed strong bonds with that team by often jumping into critical projects and delivering great results for their clients. Tina couldn't replicate this approach—PMI wasn't even her specialty—and at the start had trouble being accepted as the new leader. The collaboration analysis, however, identified key opinion leaders in the PMI group. But it wasn't just a matter of changing those individuals' minds through persuasion; Tina found in the data how she could support the subunit: first, she spotted key talent who could help fill the hole Tom's departure had left. She also identified new and promising industry verticals. Through this data-driven approach, she was able to make the unit more effective and earn their respect.

> **Quick Wins:**
>
> Here are some collaborative performance drivers you might employ in a sales organization:

- Better capture latent sales opportunities by identifying overloaded account managers. Support them with more junior high performers to develop the junior person's skills and ensure the senior has the time to engage in every promising opportunity.
- Build more reliable client relationships by identifying the account manager most important to each important client. Proactively target those individuals with retention programs.
- Optimize sales of new product lines by building direct interfaces between product managers responsible for the new product and relevant sales teams.

Tina's second main goal had been to increase the cross-selling effectiveness of this new unit. Based on project data and collaboration analytics, she looked at which consultants had participated in high-value collaborations. The results were shocking: The 10 most-connected employees had participated in collaborations that produced 60 percent of the unit's revenues—in a fast-growing unit of more than 200 employees. In fact, the top five were responsible for 40 percent of revenues. Tina decided to have promising junior colleagues shadow these star performers in critical moments such as attempts to win over new clients or when establishing cross-unit collaborations. This reduced key man risk and ensured high-potentials were trained by the best. For the top performers, the shadowing allowed them to share their expertise while being productive rather than being pulled from the front for training purposes.

Quick Wins:

Provide junior high-potentials with direct access to top performers and their routines. In the example of the sales organization: If you record your sales calls, label and distribute recordings from the top sales reps to the rest of the sales team.

Tina's cross-selling push was also supported by a change in incentives, where individual consultants' pay/bonuses depended not just on billable hours but also on performance reviews from the industry and regional units across the company. This aligned incentives, as consultants whose contributions were important to managers from other units would advance quicker in the hierarchy and receive bonus pay. Other more typical approaches to incentives included preparing concise lists of key competencies for account managers, as well as reference cases on how they used these capabilities to drive client success. Tina also built on the core team of central experts identified in the first step of the analysis to invite leaders from regional or industry groups into core team meetings. This way, key account leaders could learn more about the capabilities and people in her unit and see the potential for collaborative projects in the future.

Through all of these initiatives, Tina was able to hit the ground running and set up her fast-growing organization for success. Within six months, the number of projects in which account managers drew on her staff tripled. Billables almost doubled while client satisfaction rates increased. Collaboration analytics a year later revealed that the cohesiveness of the unit had improved dramatically.

> **Lessons Learned:**
>
> A collaboration analysis in your company allows you to understand the areas in which collaboration effectiveness can be improved significantly, and thus take targeted action to leverage these opportunities:
>
> - Who are the important players in your collaboration network? Who needs to be better integrated? Who needs to be connected with whom? How can you achieve this?
> - How well connected are employees throughout your organization? What is the intensity of their collaboration? How can you improve this?
> - What portion of your performance-critical collaborations lie outside your organization? How can you better leverage them?
> - Who are the top performers in your organization? How can you ensure that their knowledge is beneficial for training your entire workforce?
> - What is the incentive system in your organization? How can you adapt it to foster collaboration?

When Tina started, she faced a double challenge: to quickly become productive as a new leader in a unit that was essentially an internal start-up that had lost its founder. And to take the promising new unit and scale up its potential to deliver high growth. By focusing on understanding the collaboration signatures of her unit, she not only quickly developed an in-depth understanding of the inner workings of her team, but also identified places for optimizing collaboration in the unit, in turn accelerating growth.

In our experience, there are two reasons that collaboration is particularly important to scaling up promising new units. First, innovative new ventures typically operate under high degrees of change and uncertainty. In order to flourish in this kind of environment, it becomes crucially important to quickly disseminate customer insights, learnings from successful experiments, and process improvements.

Second, quick growth can imperil a unit's coordination speed and efficiency. As the ratio of experienced experts to "new blood" shifts, it becomes harder and harder to maintain onboarding quality, informal knowledge such as customer pain points, relationships to decision-makers outside the unit, and routines that drive performance. By understanding and optimizing collaboration within the unit, these core challenges in scaling up can be addressed.

Finally, by optimizing for synergies with the legacy organization, the fledgling unit can leverage the client base and competencies of more mature units, such as certain industry verticals. This addresses another core challenge for scaling up promising units in the corporate context: While they would often benefit from the resources of mature units, such as client access and technical skills, it can be very hard to realize these synergies in practice. Fast-growing units tend to have a culture that clashes with that in the legacy units—for example, when it comes to decision speed—which can make collaborations frustrating on all sides. Through identifying and positioning already successful boundary-spanning individuals, aligning incentives, and explicitly measuring these collaborations, Tina was able to overcome these challenges and leverage the legacy units to turbocharge her growth.

> **Lesson Learned:**
> Understanding and improving the collaboration patterns of your company's units is crucial to ensuring effective coordination, maintaining high quality of work, sharing important knowledge, fostering relations throughout your organization, and identifying and realizing synergies—all factors that contribute to successfully scaling a business.

5.3 Scale Faster by Scaling Lean and Orchestrating External Partners

A second potential of collaborative scaling is to stay nimbler as an organization and focus on orchestrating activities throughout your ecosystem that will help you grow quickly. Let's take a look at how one non-governmental organization (NGO) leveraged collaborative scaling principles to accelerate progress on an exciting new idea in the biomedical sector [2].

The Myelin Repair Foundation (MRF) aims to advance treatments for multiple sclerosis by helping orchestrate research and development around a promising new approach: Repairing the damage MS does to the coating substance around neurons and axons, a substance that facilitates the transmitting of electronic signals in the central nervous system.

The first phase of the MRF's work was an informal, hands-on analysis of the collaboration structure in the industry. Scott Johnson, the group's founder, attended high-profile, invitation-only networking events where leading researchers met to discuss the future of the field. Scott then reached out to forty of the researchers who had been part of these events, outlined his vision and asked for suggestions of people he should include in his initiative. Based on the responses, he constructed a first overview of the collaboration structure of the field: which labs and organizations are connected to which and how open individual teams and high-profile experts.

His analysis diagnosed the lackluster speed of progress in the field as being due to research labs mostly acting in isolation. This made sense given the incentive structure in biomedicine: An inordinate amount of resources is awarded to the group that can claim a breakthrough for itself, both in terms of academic reputation and patent protection—with the knock-on effect of it also having an enormous financial impact as new treatments come to market. Thus, labs often jealously guard important intermediate results from one another and only disclose results once the process is far enough advanced that a breakthrough is in clear sight. Progress is often only made sequentially—and slowly. (Note that similar effects of territoriality would occur in many for-profit organizations...).

> **Self-Reflection:**
> Are you shying away from external collaborations with industry peers because you want to protect your ideas? This might be hindering your ability to come up with innovative solutions in the first place.

To tackle these challenges, Scott developed a process of collaborative, parallel discovery. Through the MRF, labs in its ecosystem had access to:

- A shared technology platform.
- Real-time sharing of results rather than catching colleagues up years later.
- Monthly alignment calls.
- Designated broker staff from MRF who would liaise with individual groups, identify high-impact ideas, and facilitate mutually beneficial adoption and exchange between organizations.

This was his vision. To get it up and running, Scott had to not only create these resources but also address concerns and drive engagement. In order to build credibility in the community, he set up an advisory board populated by five high-profile researchers. He brought resources, such as funding, to the table to facilitate collaboration. And he addressed researchers' worries about how this might impact their payoff by bringing on board a team of intellectual property (IP) lawyers tasked with documenting who could lay claim to intermediate results, protecting ideas, and identifying and shielding critical IP. Scott also recruited promising researchers as co-owners of the MRF ecosystem approach, to help iterate on priorities and review results. This shared leadership handed over ownership of the project to its participants rather than focusing on MRF as the orchestrator, ensuring high engagement throughout the process.

By the end of this first phase, the results were impressive. MRF had identified and refined nineteen potential therapeutic targets. But Scott wanted to step up the non-profit's game. To do this, he launched the MRF on a new phase to professionalize and turbocharge its orchestration of the biomedical community. The goal: use collaboration analytics to find the right partners outside of researchers'/the MRF's/the MRF researchers' current network—from companies with experience bringing treatments for central nervous diseases to market (especially those who did so quickly and efficiently), to labs from adjacent research spaces and other individuals and groups overlooked in the first phase.

Together with an external partner, MRF built on rich, open-source data to construct the collaboration analysis of its entire ecosystem. Important data sources included scientific articles, patent filings, FDA approvals, press releases and data from clinical trials, and these all helped MRF develop a detailed, relatively objective view of the relevant players in the field, finding out what they worked on in the past and—crucially—with whom they had collaborated. In biotech, where almost nine in ten innovations are developed in "the long tail" of smaller players—a group that is difficult to map either intuitively or manually—this information was gold.

Through this approach, emerging players and overlooked influencers could be identified and integrated in a scalable, data-driven way. For example, it uncovered a previously overlooked Japanese biotech firm that had filed patents on a key protein target the ecosystem was beginning to explore. Rather than duplicating all the work, a collaboration was established and the labs in the network could turbocharge their own work based on this prior work.

> **Quick Win:**
> Scale your tasks through your network: For the next critical challenge, try breaking it down into a series of discrete tasks, and for each of these ask yourself: Where in my network is the relevant expertise, information, resources or support? By diffusing ownership of subtasks early and broadly, you can achieve much more and with much greater speed.

The MRF transformed its ecosystem and turbocharged the scaling up of new ideas. Scientific output has almost tripled in the ecosystem since the non-profit began its work; collaboration intensity has increased fivefold, and the jumps from scientific journal articles to clinical trials and commercially valuable patents have been galvanized. A comparison of labs that joined the MRF network and labs in a similar starting position that didn't reveals that MRF-affiliated researchers' productivity rose at about twice the rate of non-affiliated researchers.

Staying lean and achieving scale by orchestrating the broader ecosystem is an approach corporates often use in areas where there is huge technological dynamism, and where the market is still searching for dominant designs and industry standards. A good example is blockchain consortia such as Hyperledger, which brings together companies including IBM, JP Morgan Chase, Bosch, FedEx, Lenovo, Walmart, and hundreds more. Through shared underwriting of the associated cost and increasing collaborative efficiencies among partners through shared standards, this design allows organizations to achieve scale with their solutions while keeping the cost-base lean and the risks low.

> **Leader's Voice: Collaborative Scaling at Sportradar**
> *Sportradar, a market leader in sports data for media, betting, and integrity services, has impressed us for leveraging external resources to create hypergrowth. As its founder, Carsten Koerl, told us, it is all about building the right ecosystem. Only with the right partners, such as the big sports leagues (the National Football League, Major League Baseball, etc.), Sportradar can access their data and build business-relevant knowledge out of it. Large parts of the value generation come from AI companies Sportradar bought; some, for example, use computer vision to analyze a sports event with incredible precision and develop better and stronger predictions. Most of the value happens within the first second an event takes place. Therefore, the collaboration between the leagues, the media companies, the betting operators and Sportradar has to be excellent. Ecosystems with complementary partnerships for developing superior customer value are in the heart of Sportradar. They*

> were the enabler for hypergrowth before the company had its IPO at NASDAQ in 2021, and remain so.

5.4 Lead with a Focus on Collaboration to Energize Scaling

Many leaders are tempted to lead like a chess master, striving to control every move, when they should be leading like gardeners, creating and maintaining a viable ecosystem in which the organization operates.—General Stanley A. McChrystal

Let's face it: Scaling up is scary. Managing hypergrowth can become all-consuming. A big part of the challenge managers face when scaling up their units comes from the human side: How to maintain energy and a sense of community as your tiny "special forces team" is overwhelmed by new hires? How to manage the relationships between your employees to power the almost obsessive commitment needed to unleash hypergrowth? Let's take a look.

In our research for this book, we observed some of the highest-performing organizations out there to better understand the collaboration signatures driving them to this star-level of scaling up innovative initiatives. In our interviews, the people we were talking to would occasionally say something that stopped us in our tracks and forced us to re-examine our insights from a new perspective. One of these remarks was a metaphor a business unit leader employed to describe collaboration in her organization: "There is this energy in the building… I think it is because people *resonate with each other* so intensely."

In the world of physics, resonance allows you to transfer movement energy to objects without physically touching them. To put it as simply as we can, objects have an inherent natural rate of vibration. Resonance occurs when the object's natural vibration rate responds to an external stimulus of the same frequency. For us, this was a great way to illustrate the collaborative advantage we observed in high-performance organizations: People transmitting energy to each other as they resonate on the same natural rate of vibration.

Interestingly, resonance appears to be deeply ingrained in human biology. Activities that literally require us to physically resonate with each other by being in the same rhythm, such as team rowing or ballroom dancing, activate reward circuits in our brain and release oxytocin. These experiences of resonance have lasting impact on individuals and their ability to perform as a group. In all of this, collaboration is key. Research by Harvard neurologist Carl Marci into non-Western healers found these individuals often achieved remarkable results despite medically dubious approaches; Marci focuses precisely on these moments of resonance to explain the healers' effectiveness. Through measuring galvanic skin response, a physiological marker of generalized emotional arousal, he was able to point to what he calls concordances: Moments in the interaction where the physiological activity of the healer and the patient almost perfectly overlay with each other. In other words: Moments when their energy level perfectly resonates. According to Marci, these moments are a key to understanding the impact these healers have on their patients—not through their treatment, but through the relationships they are able to form [3].

While we will return later to a comprehensive discussion of how to nurture resonance in your organization, let's now take a moment to reflect on how you as a leader can model and engender resonance in your interactions with the people reporting to you. A key insight here is that resonance is much more dependent on the receiver than the sender of the message. In more practical terms: *You can do the most to build resonance in an interaction by listening, not talking*. This is especially true in key moments when your people are talking about things they feel strongly about. Such intense emotions make people feel vulnerable, and this is when resonance is built—or not, depending on your reaction. The best resonators don't just listen attentively and nod because they were told to do so in a seminar on active listening. Instead, they listen like a trampoline—not passively accepting the sender's messages but bouncing them back even higher. In the words of Roshi Givechi of design company IDEO [4], "I've found that whenever you ask a question, the first response you get is usually not the answer—it's just the first response. You have to find a lot of ways to ask the same question and approach the same question from a lot of different angles." Sakichi Toyoda, who founded Toyota Industries, is an example of how you might apply this in your work: As part of his "go and see" philosophy, he implemented the "5 Whys technique." The goal is it to find the root cause of a problem or the real reason behind a phenomenon by simply asking "why" five times. Through this exploration mindset, resonators don't passively sponge up what their conservation partner is telling them; they absorb it, yes, but then they support it and add energy to help the conversation gain velocity and altitude. Relatedly, one of the hallmarks of groups with extremely high resonance is that individuals almost never interrupt one another—the only exception being interruptions born out of shared excitement, such as in brainstorming sessions.

> **Self-Reflection:**
> Does your team resonate? In the next meeting, look for the following signs [5]:
> Close physical proximity, profuse amounts of eye contact, physical touching, lots of short energetic exchanges rather than long speeches, high levels of mixing and spontaneous interactions, few interruptions, lots of questions, active listening, a shared sense of humor, and small courtesies to each other.
> These vibrant interactions are typical indications of the resonance behind a truly high-performance organization.

Can we quantify the impact of focused, resonant collaborative advantage on organizational performance? In a comprehensive analysis of nearly 200 start-ups, researchers James Baron and Michael Hannon differentiated between three basic modes in growing a business. The first two are fairly conventional: the star model, which focuses on hiring the best people, and the professional model, which focuses on hiring around specific skill sets. Baron and Hannon's third model, commitment model, is more unusual. It centers around building strong personal emotional bonds across the organization—or, in other words, it prioritizes nurturing resonant collaborations in the organization, even at the cost of other valid HR goals.

The research essentially asked whether, when hiring, you should look for the best people generally, for specific skill sets or for personal commitment. How would the commitment model fare compared with the other two when it came to a company's performance? The researchers found that it consistently outperformed the other two models. Start-ups focused on the commitment model were three times more likely to achieve an IPO than those that embraced the other two models, and were much more likely to survive market crashes and economic crises.

An even more pointed demonstration directly compares the importance of the collaboration signatures of a group versus the individual skills of the group members. Researchers from MIT had groups of engineers engage in technical problem-solving challenges. They then organized a little "horse race" between two algorithms trying to predict which groups would be the most successful. The first of these algorithms was fed all the relevant information about the individual group members. The second algorithm, in contrast, had no information about the skills or background of the individual engineers. It did, however, have access to the interaction patterns between group members; it could thus base its predictions on a data-driven understanding of the collaboration signature of the group.

The study found the second algorithm clearly superior to the first and predicted the relative successes of the groups. The collaboration signature of the group was more telling, when it came to group performance, than all the individual attributes of the group members combined [6]. In the words of the lead researcher: "Group problem-solving ability is mostly independent of individual intelligence and emerges from the connections between individuals."

Interestingly, the features of the collaboration signature that the algorithm used for its predictions almost directly reflect the resonance of the group: many very short contributions, rather than a few long ones, produced a large number of ideas; interactions were dense, continuous, overlapping cycles of contribution and response; the responses were very short—less than one second, the likes of "good" or "what?"—and there were very similar levels of turn taking by the different group members. Together, these indicators of a resonant collaboration signature determined more than half of the performance variation across all groups.

Deep Dive: Collaborative Resonance and the Pink Panthers [7]

Over the course of the early 2000s, a group that came to be known as the Pink Panthers conducted a series of daring and incredibly successful heists at some of the world's most exclusive jewelry stores. In conducting their sallies, they employed a combination of ingenuity and ruthless speed of execution. For example, in a 2007 burglary in Tokyo four male Panthers dressed up as wealthy middle-aged women, complete with wigs and expensive dresses, in order to rob a Harry Winston store of jewelry worth $105 million. They used Audi sports cars as battering rams in order to breach an exclusive store in Dubai, escaped by speedboat from a heist in St. Tropez, and made off in a chauffeured Bentley after a robbery in London. Each caper was fluently executed, normally running at fewer than 45 seconds from start to finish. The journalist Daniel Coyle, who featured the group in one of his books, quotes a criminologist who describes their work as "artistry." How did they manage this? Were they highly trained professionals, ex-military or police, just lucky fools?

Naturally, the international team of police officers tasked with apprehending the Panthers assumed that crimes that appeared so professionally executed, taking place in the limelight, moreover, could only be committed by extremely well-trained and well-funded individuals. They knew the thieves had roots in the former Yugoslavia, the most popular theory was that the Panthers were former Serbian special forces building on large resources from sponsors at home. In fact, the world eventually learned that the Panthers were a self-governed and self-assembling group of deeply ordinary people. Some were middle-class, such as a lawyer; some were athletes, such as a former member of the Serbian national youth basketball team. They didn't have sponsors back in Serbia, nor did they boast any specialized training or equipment. What they could rely on was a deeply resonant collaboration signature.

As it turns out, most of the Panthers were friends from childhood, having grown up in one of three towns. Havana Marking, who directed a documentary about the group, says: "The experience of going through the communist regime and then the free-for-all nightmare of the war that followed, that really bonded them." The indicators of that bond are evident in their work. Video footage of the robberies makes apparent the physical rhythms they share: They move fluently through the stores, extremely coordinated. They know exactly when and where to go without explicit communication.

Investigators later learned that, in the preparation of their heists, they lived together for several weeks in the city. While there usually was a leader, he never issued commands; instead, the individual Panthers would work together, helping one another in preparation. No wonder, perhaps, since if any individual failed in a task, the group would fail, and land in prison. Finally, the members of the group also displayed immense loyalty in an environment not known for loyal characters. When one Panther was apprehended in France and sent to prison, others soon broke him out.

Despite having very few of the resources experts deemed they must have to pull off these heists, the Pink Panthers succeeded. No professional thieves among them, no wealthy sponsors behind them—but a deeply resonant collaboration signature between them: this turned out to be the winning formula in the world of jewelry thievery, much more than any assemblage of highly trained individuals.

5.5 Employ Nudges to Help Your Scale-Up Team Resonate

You can't usually ensure that your employees have grown up together, and even forcing them to cohabitate for weeks on projects would be a questionable management practice. What, then, are viable strategies for systematically developing a resonant collaboration signature?

Let's take a look at a project at Bank of America in answer to these questions. The setting—the bank's customer service call centers—allows us to put a fairly precise dollar amount on the value of collaborative advantage [8]. Offering customer support through a call center would not appear at first glance to be a team activity. It requires efficiency and productivity, and each employee completes his work very much in parallel with colleagues. The center thus provides a conservative test of the notion of collaborative advantage over mere "teamwork" or other established categories: if it's true there, it should be true anywhere.

Since most call centers are run as cost centers, average call handling time (AHT) is the most important productivity measure there. Essentially, AHT dominates the running cost of the call center while taking into account how many client requests are serviced. One analysis of one of BofA's call centers found that reducing AHT there by just 5 percent would save the bank roughly $1 million a year; rolling this out across the organization would of course have saved multiples more. An initial collaboration analysis of the interaction patterns confirmed what you probably already suspected: A resonant collaboration signature in a group of call center agents was strongly correlated with their performance, as measured by AHT. In fact, two simple indicators of resonance predicted roughly one-third of the variation across groups in dollar productivity in the call center.

With this insight in hand, BofA's/the call center's management decided to try to increase the collaborative advantage within the groups of call center agents using simple nudges. For example, employees tended to take their coffee breaks one at a time, in line with typical call center policy: this way, the service remained available even if a few employees were away from their desks. However, the call center in which the project took place was huge, and it was possible to shift call loads between groups rather than within teams. Team coffee breaks, then, became a simple way to increase the number of informal interactions between team members.

These sorts of opportunities to mix and engage with one another increased the resonance within the teams. This in turn led to sharp increases in AHT, demonstrating the link between collaborative advantage and productivity. After evaluating the results of these experimental changes, management converted the break structures for all employees. The prospect of productivity increases worth $15 million a year in just this one call center was too good to pass up.

> **Lessons Learned:**
> Collaborative advantage can turbocharge even autonomous work (like customer support).
> Relatively simple nudges (like re-designing breaks) can transform collaboration signatures.

What might the mechanisms be for this first phenomenon? In contrast to prior examples set in start-ups, strategy departments, and criminal syndicates (the Pink Panthers), call center work is essentially an individual performance. If the prior examples were soccer matches, the call center is like a relay race. In a soccer match, it is clear that how team members interact affects group performance, whereas a relay race looks, at first, like an instance of group performance simply being the sum of individual's part. Why, then, is collaboration also so important here? Two key functions of collaborative advantage help us understand: social learning and social energizing.

Let's start with social learning. A few chapters ago, we pointed to the benefits of learning from your peers for a wide range of human activities. Managing relational learning in your organization, particularly informal relational learning, requires that you be aware of a key distinction: acquiring new knowledge versus learning new skills. When we talked about ensuring that your organization excels at sensing innovative opportunities, we mostly discussed how people become aware of new ideas, trends, and opportunities. How, in other words, they take on new knowledge, one component of developing collaborative advantage. A common pitfall here, we found, was getting trapped in an echo chamber, since groups of similar people often reinforce old mental models even as the world around them changes.

So far, so good. But in the context of seizing opportunities that have been sniffed out through good sensing, and executing on them, we are mostly concerned with the transmission of best practices—the tricks of the trade and the behavior scripts for handling challenges in one's daily work. These are all related to learning *skills*. Consequently, this type of social learning is not so much driven by how much your collaboration signature connects people who are different from each other, but by how much it connects people who are similar or close to each other. Informal exchanges between co-workers in the same team, such as in the Bank of America case, are a crucial vector for this social learning. And putting in the work to ensure these happen pays off: a cohesive, resonant collaboration signature allows for individuals to fluently transmit skills and best practices across the group, driving productivity and execution.

A second outcome of collaborative advantage, social energizing, adds to our understanding of why even a call center will benefit from a resonant collaborative signature. This type of collaboration energizes individuals to commit to and persevere in their work in a way that purely individual incentives can seldom match. This effect is on top of and independent from practical help, or learning from peers. And it doesn't take much to trigger this energizing mechanism. For example, in a classic study, individual workers were presented with a difficult cognitive task [9]. After two minutes they received a tip from "Steve," a colleague who had done the challenge earlier and wanted to help. In reality, there was no Steve and the tip the researchers manufactured was utterly useless for completion of the task. Still, workers who received the tip were more motivated, readier to persevere, and more likely to engage in similar challenges in the future than those in the control group.

This effect will clearly be even stronger in a truly resonant collaboration built on real relationships. But we see that just the smallest signal of support is enough to start trigger the energizing effects the collaborative advantage. Scientists can watch this happening in the brain: neurological scanning in real time allows us to see that when people receive resonant relational signals, the function of the Amygdala changes. Normally, this part of the limbic system serves as a threat response system and its activation is associated with worried rumination rather than focused performance. But in a setting with a cohesive collaboration signature, it changes its function and Amygdala activations are associated with greater likelihood of social engagement and more energized individual behavior.

We will discuss the energizing function of the collaborative advantage in much greater detail in part 4, when we focus on the topic of business transformation.

> **Lessons Learned:**
> A resonant collaboration signature drives performance by increasing coordination, social learning (best-practice exchange), and social energizing (the motivational effect of peer support).

Let's quickly return to the Bank of America case and highlight a second important take-away: how banal an intervention can be and yet still nurture collaborative advantage. Aligning coffee breaks hardly seems a revolutionary idea, yet the business impact speaks for itself. The genius of this approach is not in finding nudges that create more opportunities for collaboration–; it is in mapping the collaboration signature of your organization to your strategic priorities, and finding out where targeted changes to collaboration patterns can improve the overall flow of resources and ideas through the social nervous system of your organization.

> **Lessons Learned:**
> It's more important to be precise about where to increase collaboration than creative about how to increase it.

The seeming contradiction between the simplicity of the nudge and the enormous impact also points to a fundamental truth about collaborative advantage: While the emergent social interaction patterns that govern collaborative advantage are relatively complex, the underlying forces shaping it are pretty simple. Humans are not alone in this; many seemingly complex social patterns emerge from deceptively simple social signals.

Consider the example of starling flocks. Starlings are relatively small, ordinary looking songbirds. What makes them remarkable is their adaptability as a social group. When a flock of starlings is threatened by a predator such as a falcon, the entire flock reacts in a fluent and visually stunning way. The flock changes its shape from instant to instant, forming giant hourglasses, spirals, and tendrils—whatever it takes to defend against the predator. Even as the falcon attacks one part of the flock, starlings thousands of birds away react to protect the flock. Initially, researchers were perplexed by this complex social behavior, which is called murmuration, but came to understand it is the result of simple behavior at the individual-bird level. Each starling reacts to the changes in flight behavior of the six other birds closest to it. Since each starling shares the same simple rules and closely observes the others, the entire flock is capable of complex adaptive reactions which no single starling could orchestrate. It is the product of focused attention on a small set of key signals.

Similarly, and with the right collaboration signature, each individual in an organization will react to a fairly simple set of social signals from their immediate environment, but the effect will be complex patterns of innovation, scaling and transformation. This is great news for you as a manager: It means that by engineering relatively simple social signals in a targeted manner, you can affect huge social changes in your organization.

> **Self-Reflection:**
> What is limiting the flow of resources and ideas through your business? Not enough collaboration between the right people (quantity) or not the right kind of collaboration (quality)?

References

In order to keep the book lean enough to comfortably be read on a plane, we have listed the full references on the companion website for your convenience. If you want to dig deeper, please check them out here:

1. Collaborative-advantage.org/references-scaling/1.
2. Collaborative-advantage.org/references-scaling/2.
3. Collaborative-advantage.org/references-scaling/3.
4. Collaborative-advantage.org/references-scaling/4.
5. Collaborative-advantage.org/references-scaling/5.
6. Collaborative-advantage.org/references-scaling/6.
7. Collaborative-advantage.org/references-scaling/7.
8. Collaborative-advantage.org/references-scaling/8.
9. Collaborative-advantage.org/references-scaling/9.

6

Managing Growth Challenges Through Collaborative Scaling

> *Brilliant people tend to think that ideas move mountains. But in the real world, bulldozers move mountains.*
> —Peter Drucker

6.1 Increase Collaborations in a Targeted Manner

At that Bank of America call center, management merely had to increase the quantity of informal interaction within a tribe of similar colleagues in order to increase productivity. It changed processes to facilitate informal in-group interactions. But we've seen nudges employed earlier in these pages, too. For example, in the case of the eToro trading platform, echo chambers were broken up mainly by reducing the number of interactions that took place within an echo chamber. In the case of the bank, productivity was increased through an increase in interaction quantity within groups.

Here's another example [10]. Halliburton is one of the world's biggest oil field service companies, with about 55,000 employees worldwide. As one of the premier professional service providers to the petroleum and energy industry, with operations in over 70 countries, a central challenge at the company is developing and maintaining the high level of expertise needed to execute their business across geographic divisions.

One of the company's core offerings is the design, manufacture, and installation of equipment that produces hydrocarbons from newly drilled oil and gas wells. The final phase of this process in particular entails huge complexity and variability, as the equipment has to be tightly aligned with the well's operational parameters. As the completion of the well develops, there is huge dynamism to these parameters. A crucial focus of the business unit that manages this offering is to reduce nonproducing time, which can substantially affect profitability due to penalty contracts.

The ability to quickly pool and transmit expertise across boundaries is key to the operational success of these complicated projects. For example, after coming up against a problem in the final project phase of a deep-water well project in West Africa, the unit was able to connect globally distributed experts so quickly that not only the specific challenge was solved but three other projects, set to be completed within the next 24 hours, were adapted at the last minute to avoid running into the same problem—saving important customers millions of dollars.

Let's consider the complexity of this process from a collaborative perspective: After identifying a problem, a project leader has to find and mobilize the right experts to solve it. These experts, who are presumably busy on their own projects, have to quickly assess the problem and contribute their specific expertise to a virtual, likely asynchronous conversation with other experts to find a solution. This solution then has to be tested and implemented in dynamic interaction with the local team. In addition, someone in this process must be aware of other projects who run similar risks, inform the people responsible for these, and guide them through the necessary adaptations. Finally, all of this has to take place in an incredibly small window of time given the financial implications of nonproductive time for assets in this sector.

No wonder Halliburton invests an enormous amount of time and energy into their ability to dynamically pool and deploy expertise across projects. Collaboration analytics of the global expert network allowed the unit responsible for the final phases of equipment installation to optimize its underlying collaboration signatures to ensure exactly that sort of coordination occurs. The results of the initial analysis are shown here. In this visualization, every expert is represented by a circle, and the collaboration between two experts represented by a line connecting the circles (Fig. 6.1).

Not surprisingly, and similar to many other organizations, experts working in the same regions are tightly connected with one another. Connections across regions exist but are much sparser.

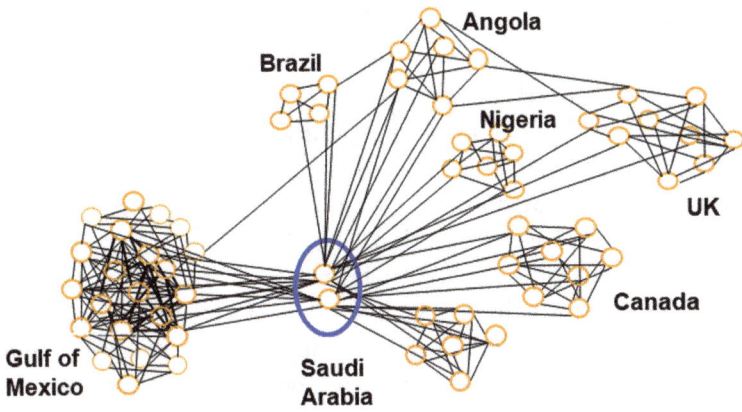

Fig. 6.1 Global Expert Network at Halliburton, stylized for clarity and simplicity

What can you, as an executive, do with this sort of analysis? First, it allows you to replace a naïve "more is better" approach with data-driven, targeted solutions to optimize collaboration patterns. Imagine your Chief Logistics Officer proposing that, to improve delivery times, more truck drivers be hired indiscriminately across the organization. You would probably ask for the logistics officer's data-based reasoning, showing where inventory is being held up, where drivers are scarce, and so on. But when it comes to the logistics of transmitting and dynamically deploying intangible human resources such as expertise, many organizations are fine winging it based on gut feeling and broad initiatives.

> **Self-Reflection:**
>
> Think about your organization's expert network: how tight are cross-region and cross-unit connections? Is expertise and knowledge transparently deployed across your organization to the point of highest return on investment?

In the case of Halliburton, collaboration analytics pointed to a crucial bottleneck in the Gulf of Mexico. The experts based there serve as brokers and indirectly connect experts across all geographical regions. If you remember the case of the multinational asset manager from a few chapters back, this type of brokerage is an essential ingredient in innovation. However, for a group of Halliburton's size, it is hugely inefficient to rely on just two brokers. Operations in the Gulf of Mexico had developed novel best practices and halved the cost of poor quality in the year prior to the analysis. However, in other regions, cost of poor quality had *increased* by 13 percent over the same period.

Clearly, a transfer of best practices and operational support throughout the network wasn't working. One reason might have been that well-connected experts were often tapped for repetitive and mundane challenges from the field rather than being able to focus on capturing, codifying, and transmitting best practices. On the surface, these and similar issues may not have seemed connected (and in most organizations would have been tackled by completely different managers). The collaboration analytics, however, revealed them to be symptoms of the same challenge: bottlenecks in resource transmission through overreliance on a limited number of overloaded brokers.

Based on these insights, Halliburton was able to devise a targeted approach of strategically increasing collaboration in some parts of the network and decreasing it in others. For example, targeted job rotations across regions established direct collaborative relationships between hitherto only indirectly connected regions. Less connected experts were brought in touch with field operators, reducing the load of repetitive work the most central experts had been forced to undertake. These experts were, in turn, given more resources and a broader mandate to focus on their role as brokers, engaging in knowledge collection and dissemination across the network.

Just nine months later, a formal evaluation clearly documented the effectiveness of this targeted approach. The average time it took for the expert network to deliver a solution to a problem was reduced by a full order of magnitude, from thirty days to just three. Meanwhile, across all regions, customer dissatisfaction was reduced by a quarter, cost of poor quality reduced by two-thirds, new product revenue increased by 22 percent, and operational productivity improved by more than 10 percent. Understanding and actively managing for collaborative advantage is not merely a topic for HR; it is not about increasing job satisfaction or team spirit. Rather, it is about optimizing the hidden engine behind successful execution—and it produces tangible business outcomes (Fig. 6.2).

> **Quick Win:**
>
> Improve collaborative scaling both by thinking about the parts played by both well-connected and more isolated employees:
>
> - For well-connected employees: Manage overload, and make sure to identify and reward collaboration.
> - For more isolated employees: Integrate newcomers as well as remote workers. Take ownership of getting them in touch with the important people so they can better develop their own network.

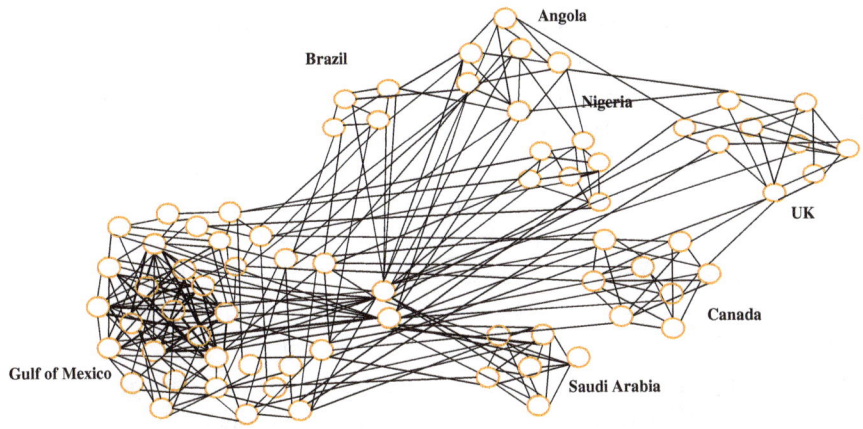

Fig. 6.2 Global Expert Network at Halliburton after changes, stylized for clarity and simplicity

Many high-performing organizations already implicitly make investment decisions that aim to increase this type of informal interaction frequency. For example, the lavish benefits employees receive at premier tech companies such as Google or Facebook can be understood from this perspective: Providing excellent options for dinner on the company campus, as well as sports and personal care facilities, provides a powerful incentive for employees to engage with each other informally and built resonant relationships. The resulting execution-edge of a resonant workforce provides a highly favorable return on these investments, particularly in companies that derive competitive advantage from the human capital of their workforce.

> **Lessons Learned:**
> Overtaxed experts often become bottlenecks for boundary-spanning collaborations. Targeted job rotations can be one tool to diversify collaboration and improve performance.

Consider the example of a specialized management tool piloted in mixed-culture work groups. Here, the collaboration signature of work groups consisting both of Japanese and American participants was analyzed [11]. Similar to other examples, the analysis revealed that the best-performing groups were operating to the same rhythm—as measured by body movement, tone of voice, and share of speaking time, and more. Based on this analysis, the group members received a visual representation of the collaboration signature in their group (much like the image associated with the Halliburton analysis). Over time, this feedback led to more resonant collaboration signature patterns, in turn increasing group performance.

We see here the intimate relationship between a data-driven understanding of an organization's collaboration signature and the management of collaborative advantage. And we see that data need not only be used to guide managers about where to nudge, but can serve as a nudge in and of itself. We have found in a variety of projects that stylized visual representations of collaborative advantage patterns, combined with accessible explanations of their meaning, are a great way to urge people toward more functional patterns. The visual representation serves as a material artifact that makes dysfunctional patterns tangible and thus creates urgency for change. Consider the social dynamic when a company board sees a visional representation of a clearly isolated business unit: In our experience, this energizes people to change things up. And when the feedback is provided consistently over time, it can serve as a steering indicator to guide the self-regulation of the organization's collaboration signature. Nor must you choose one approach or another: the data-visualization nudge can be combined with other nudges in forms we have described above.

> **Quick Win:**
>
> Here are some easy-to-implement approaches for increasing informal interaction frequency:
>
> - Provide on-site incentives (sports, food, etc.) to foster informal exchanges between employees
> - Use visualizations of a team's collaboration patterns and regular feedback to nudge self-regulated changes in their interactions

6.2 Improve Quality of Collaborations

The quality of interactions is also an important determinant of an organization's collaboration signature. This is especially true when capitalizing on collaborative advantage with scaling up as your goal. As we have seen, being able to do this depends hugely on how resonant the collaboration signature is in your organization.

How do you increase the quality of interactions systemically? Bridgewater Associates' Dot Collector, discussed in Chapter 3, worked well. In this case, the main goal of the nudge was to reduce groupthink and trigger self-reflection and broader outreach among the group members. Similar to the visual feedback tool we discussed above, it was a data-driven solution that transformed the collaboration signature of the group.

Another helpful approach is focusing on creating shared, personally meaningful experiences. These can address the quality of the relationships between close peers but also between central stakeholders who might not ordinarily work closely with one another.

Take, for example, a fundraising call center working for a major American university. The center's employees were tasked with persuading wealthy individuals to fund scholarship programs [12]. As anybody who has ever worked cold-calling customers can tell you, this is difficult and often frustrating work. The rejection rate for the call center team stood at a towering 93 percent. To motivate employees and increase performance, the university had tried several "classical" interventions focused on the individuals, such as prizes or contests. Each had failed.

Now think back to the case of the Bank of America call center project, when we discussed the energizing function of collaborative advantage. Meaningful social interactions invigorate and motivate individuals, and the Wharton team working with the university fundraising call center kept this in mind when they organized visits from scholarship recipients. Each visit only lasted about five minutes. The students didn't share complex ideas or give inspirational talks. Instead, each simply told his or her own story: Here's where I come from. Here's what the money you raised means to me.

Through this relational experience of engaging with people who could show the positive impact the call center employees were having on their lives, the abstract task of raising donor money became imbued with social meaning. This energized the workers—and more than doubled the average time spent per phone call. And it showed up in tangible, dollar values: Over the next month, donations increased by 172 percent. As in so many other cases we have we shared, here there was no change in incentives, systems, or training. Just an explicit use of collaborative advantage to energize employees through meaningful, human connection. And the results were transformative.

Why was it so important to put a face on the work the employees were engaged in? Had they not realized their work was important and meaningful? In order to answer that question, we have to consider human psychology and evolution. The part of our brains that manages emotions and motivation, the limbic system, is fairly old in evolutionary terms, and the way it guides our behavior is optimized for the environment in which it developed. During this time, survival and reproduction was to an overwhelming degree dependent on our ability to function and cooperate within our tribe. Hunting, child-rearing, almost every activity required social cooperation. By doing things that were of direct value to other members of our tribe, our ancestors increased their social status and ability to obtain this kind of cooperation from others. Since this was so crucial to survival, and the ability to reproduce, we are descended from individuals whose limbic systems reacted strongly to this type of direct social feedback. As such, these socially minded experiences basically light a fire in our brains, saying: This is great, keep doing this! And direct relational experience says this much more loudly than the abstract knowledge that we are doing good, which is processed in a different part of the brain.

> **Lesson Learned:**
> Maximizing the quality of interactions your employees have with peers and other stakeholders can be as or more important than the quantity. Positive feedback and appreciation are key—not only from within your organization but also from external parties affected by your employees' work.

Making contact with customers or other focal stakeholders can be a great way for companies to use relational experiences to energize their employees. Alas, not every company works as directly with customers who can relate the personal, transformative importance of the work the employees do to their lives. What about companies which deal in commodities or produce machine parts? What about organizations that are dealing in systemically valuable rather than personally valuable goods?

These groups have another, perhaps even more effective, pathway to explore: focusing on how their employees make life better for their colleagues. Let's take an extreme case to highlight how this collaboration signature works [13].

Most of us our jobs don't ask us to risk life and limb for our colleagues. How, then, is this story relevant to our organizations? Many high-performance organizations will rank their values and priorities, and while it management theory places a lot of importance today on "customer obsession" and placing the customer first, we have found that organizations with truly resonating collaboration signature always name the same number one value and priority: Taking care of each other. They see their colleagues as family, and their answers to the question posed to Johnny Bravo would be the same. Why go above and beyond for your colleagues? Because they would have done it for me.

How do you build the kind of collaborative advantage that creates this motivation? A good starting point is building trust between your employees. And a primary driver of trust is shared experiences of intimacy and vulnerability. How, then, can you nurture these experiences among your employees?

Let's take inspiration from the WIPRO call center in Bangalore, India. It's a nice setting as call centers go, with great benefits for the standards of the local labor market. And yet it still couldn't manage to keep employees on. Each year, between 50 and 70 percent of workers left and had to be re-recruited, ramping up recruiting and training costs and causing productivity losses. The company tried several initiatives to reduce attrition, such as raising salaries, increasing perks, and shouting about its award-winning status as a top employer—but to no avail.

Frustrated, Wipro executives contracted the help of a group of researchers [14]. These researchers designed a one-hour intervention at the onboarding of new hires, focused squarely on engendering collaborative advantage between employees. After seven months, new hires who went through the intervention were more than two times as likely to still work for the call center than the from a control group that experienced the traditional onboarding.

The intervention was fairly straightforward: new hires were asked an escalating stream of personal questions, and encouraged to share their answers with others. These included questions like, "What is unique about you that leads to your happiest times and best performances at work?" This, in fact, is a variation of classical social-psychological procedure called the experimental generation of interpersonal closeness. Behind this unwieldy name hides a fairly simple idea: Close bonds are formed in a reciprocal process of increasing investments and intimacy: from small talk to deeper conversations, on to invitations and shared activities, and finally to relying on each other and trusting each other. Moments of vulnerability, in which people share slightly more than they feel totally comfortable with, and then have this vulnerability rewarded by an empathetic reaction and a reciprocal opening up by others, are crucial to create this shared bond of trust. If you think back to the healers we discussed earlier in this chapter, this follows the same principle: Creating moments of resonance. The procedure systematically engineers this process through a guided set of questions and instructions. The WIPRO case documents the viability of this approach in a corporate setting as a way of nurturing a more resonant collaboration signature, in turn energizing employees and increasing their persistence.

> **Self-Reflection:**
> Think about your onboarding process: how many personal interaction moments (instead of purely professional ones) do you design between new hires and their peers in their first two months?

6.3 Vulnerability as a Leader Helps You Nurture Resonance

> I was asked whether I would fire an employee who just made a mistake which cost the company $600,000. No, I replied, I just spent $600,000 training him.—Thomas Watson

On top of lateral relations between peers, vulnerability is also a crucial lever for the collaboration signature between leaders and their teams. Especially in times of crisis, conventional wisdom for many leaders holds that they should project strength and a sense of orientation for the employees: Trust me, I know what to do, do what I say and I'll get us through this crisis. This, however, might not always be the best approach.

We can see this in the tale of United Airlines Flight 232 [15], wherein a situation built with all the ingredients for the complete collapse of a group under pressure. That is to say, lives were at stake, the challenges were huge, and the group included new members. Of course, no one knew this when the flight took off from Denver, headed to Chicago.

At 3.16 p.m., an explosion shattered the aircraft, taking out one of three engines and the hydraulic control system through which the plane was controlled. The plane started to tilt uncontrollably. Incidents like these are called catastrophic failures in the industry. Nobody trains for them, for two reasons: First, catastrophic failures are very rare. And second, they are always fatal. Indeed, as part of the investigation of the incident later, the National Transportation Safety Board simulated the problem with 29 experienced crews. All 29 failed to land the plane, resulting in the simulated loss of all 285 passengers—every single time.

On board Flight 232, from the moment of the explosion, the crew was desperately trying to come up with solutions. The pilot and his co-pilot were working with engineers from United to isolate the problem, while coordinating their mostly involuntary flight path with air traffic control and preparing emergency staff at the ground. In addition, a pilot trainer from United who happened to be on the plane as a passenger had joined them in the cockpit. None of these people knew each other beforehand, and they faced a whole array of almost impossible problems. Incredibly, they figured out how to "steer" the plane by changing power distributions to the two remaining engines over the next few hours. They managed to reach Sioux City airport and land the plane in a semi-controlled crash on the runway. They saved the lives of the large majority of passengers survived, and the entire crew.

To learn from this example, look at the interactions in the cockpit between the spontaneously assembled crisis team. Instead of projecting confidence and authority, the members quickly shared vulnerable exchanges. Instead of telling the captain what to do, the first words of the pilot trainer were: "Tell me what you want, and I'll help you." Instead of saying "I got this," the captain continuously reinforced another message: "I have no idea what is going on or how to fix it. Can you help?" The leader shared his own vulnerability as well as ownership of the solution of the problem equally across the room. This enabled a uniquely effective interaction pattern.

Instead of one person taking charge, the communication in the cockpit took a very different shape. People shared quick notifications, half-sentences about their observations ("Got brakes now," "300 and descending") to keep the other members in the loop. The second feature of the communication were open-ended questions, asking for help and input ("How do we get the landing gear down? Anybody got ideas?"). An egalitarian interaction pattern, highly reminiscent of our indicators of a resonant collaboration signature, saved lives. To achieve this in the midst of a crisis, quickly and among an unfamiliar group, is impressive. And the trigger of this emergent collaborative advantage was the captain sharing his vulnerability and asking for support.

> **Self-Reflection:**
> How often do you as a leader make it clear to your reports that you don't know the answer to something and depend on their creative input to figure it out?

Leaders' Voices: Resonant Leadership in Crisis: Learnings from COVID-19

How do these principles apply in the corporate context? In order to find out, we analyzed exemplary leadership at the onset of the covid-19 pandemic.

When we asked managers about their priorities in the crisis, we always got the same answer: "Our first priority is to care for our employees." And indeed, employees were under a lot of pressure. In addition to immediate health concerns, Covid also caused economic insecurity as well as stress from the isolation of social distancing or working from home while caring for children whose schools were closed. How did leaders address these worries and stresses, above and beyond ensuring that on-site working conditions were safe?

Tangible commitments are a crucial way for managers to provide support and increase safety for their employees in the face of economic uncertainty. For example, despite huge financial pressure in his sector, the CEO of Sportradar decided to pay out all bonuses immediately at the onset of the pandemic. Novartis postponed a long-planned restructuring. Insurance company Zurich demonstrated its trust for the employees by eliminating all requirements for documenting sick leave or leave to care for sick family members. It also made a public commitment to continuing to pay employees for the duration of the pandemic who were not able to fulfill their role from home. By walking the walk making expensive commitments to their employees, these managers communicated the desire to get through the crisis together: If leaders make clear they are in it for the long run, their employees will be, too.

In addition, many leaders supported employees in dealing with the non-economic stresses brought about by social distancing. Indeed, a review in the Lancet reported negative effects of quarantine measures ranging from confusion and anger to post-traumatic stress symptoms. Resonant leaders also offered support here. For example, Novartis set up systems to share childcare responsibilities across workers in the same quarantine zones, as well as expanding their subscriptions for online learning services from their employees to their entire families. Newly developed physical and mental well-being apps (Novartis) and ramp-ups in employee assistance programs (Zurich) are further examples of how leaders lent support to employees.

Demonstrating support for employees does not only fulfill responsibilities to a central stakeholder of the company. In addition, it creates an environment of psychological safety and engagement, which are both crucial to guiding an organization through a crisis. If a leader demonstrates that he has the employee's back, then he can ask the employee to do the same.

Leaders also started distributing ownership for managing the Covid crisis across their organizations.

"You will not survive this if only the management steers the company," said the chief executive of Sportradar. Building on the safety and engagement created

through the support the company had offered its employees at the start, managers invited employees to share their insights, decisions, and motivations. "In the crisis, leadership has moved from command and control to a more consultative model of leadership" (CHRO; Zurich).

How to draw employees' input? Managers clearly stated that they did not have all the answers. "The situation is so complex and unprecedented that we cannot delegate it to global experts. The employees who are closest to the issues and to the customers are in the best position to assess what is needed," (Novartis). While some managers communicated this more aggressively than others—"The intelligence of this company is now in the base, not in the board," said the CEO of Marquard Media Group—we we saw even highly traditional organizations open up to insights and ideas from outside the leadership. "We see new people step forward with creative ideas we didn't really have on the radar before" (CEO, Tchibo, a popular German chain of coffee shops and retail).

Aside from making clear that this sort of input was welcome, senior leaders opened up channels through which these insights could reach the C-Suite. For example, Marquard Media Group hosted daily deep dive calls to deal with Covid-related challenges. On these calls, employees from all levels of the corporate hierarchy were represented, from the Group CEO all the way down to operational colleagues. At Tchibo, the CEO spent most of his time in calls with the business units, and then communicated their ideas and suggestions to the board.

Beyond inviting insights, companies also empowered individual decision-making at lower levels of the hierarchy: "You can really only adapt fast enough in a distributed model of decision-making" (CHRO, Zurich). Novartis aimed to operate as a "school of fish, where everybody has been empowered to make decisions and is required to share his experiences and learning,." Simply delegating decision-making authority down the hierarchy is not enough to make this approach work. Instead, alignment across functions and locations through lateral communication channels and providing an overarching framework of where to go from the senior leadership are also needed.

Companies built on this to seize opportunities. "This is an opportunity to digitalize the Marquard Media Group even faster than before, taking three steps for one," said the CEO. Investing in new digital technologies that increased efficiency and reduced costs was a focus for many companies we observed (Zühlke, Sportradar, Marquard Media Group, Tchibo). The CEO of Weidmann, the medical and electrical devices maker, emphasized that, because they provided critical components to Roche's Covid-19 tests, "this provide[d] purpose which brings all our employees together to one mission—independent—of the country and place they are working, independent of home office or factory." In addition, internal processes were shifting. "Remote work is here to stay. Many companies will look at things such as travel policies with fresh eyes, and operate in a much more sustainable way in the future" (CHRO, Zurich).

None of this was a one-way street. Leaders asked employees to go above and beyond during the crisis. Just as the companies made sacrifices to help their employees through, employees were called upon to give their most and make sacrifices. Examples include short-term work, flexibility over vacation time, and taking on work that lay outside their normal responsibilities.

Through such activities, the companies were able to open new and creative potential for managing these crises—and even for managing in normal times.

As the chief executive of Marquard Media Group put it, "a crisis is a terrible thing to waste."

We were consistently impressed with the creativity and focus companies employed to identify and develop new opportunities out of the crisis.

Opportunities were created early through the re-deployment of existing capabilities. The CEO of Marquard Media Group told us about how he was inspired by the story of LVMH repurposing one of their factories to produce hand sanitizer. With this in mind, he promoted a marketing expert to a leadership position and tasked this person with creating a media campaign helping people understand how the business world was responding to Covid. Sportradar repositioned their engineering talent toward E-Sports offerings after most physical sports leagues canceled their seasons builded new offerings for a quarantined populace. Zühlke co-developed new professional services offerings since their customers were faced with disruptions in their internal processes. Tchibo capitalized on now underpriced marketing and distribution opportunities for their products. Zurich developed new financial products to support people hit hardest by the crisis.

If life was a Hollywood movie, the script for the future would be clear: In the face of crisis, the (unusually good-looking) protagonists come together. One gives a rousing speech and everybody thinks about what they are fighting for. Then, most likely through a sudden strike of ingenuity, the crisis is overcome.

In reality, this coming together proved difficult in times of social distancing. What were the success factors we observed allowing leaders to adapt to the crisis?

Empathetic Leadership: As the first success factor, empathetic leadership refers to the direct, emotional engagement between the leadership and the employees. This is not only crucially important for a seamless vertical flow of information across hierarchy levels, but also is the basis for the engaging and motivating nature of crisis leadership.

During the onset of the crisis, many organizations focused on visual communication to do this, with senior managers sharing pictures from their home offices (as was the case with Novartis) and video messages (at Zurich) instead of only text-based communication. Virtual townhalls to address the current situation as well as share worries and plans were also an important tool; in fact, the CEO of Sportradar hosted a visual townhall on a Sunday evening which was attended by more than 80 percent of the employees—some of whom were in completely different time zones. The CEO of Tchibo referred to his job amid Covid as "Chief

Empathy Officer" and stepped back from a formal position in the crisis task force to focus his time on direct calls with the business unit leaders. Zurich required all managers to regularly, personally call all their team members to keep the level of engagement high.

A second success factor was decision speed: fast but not hectic decision-making determined the speed of adaptability. In order to face the unprecedented volatility of the crisis environment, companies radically increased the speed of their decision-making.

One way this can be done is through streamlining important decisions through crisis task forces. These were usually comprised of members of the management board, with support from the most affected functions, such as HR and Legal. Frequency of meetings for these task forces ranged from twice a day to twice a week in our sample, but in any case provided a much faster route to alignment and implementation of critical decisions.

In addition, to reduce the load on the task force and increase decision speed, even more local bodies were empowered to make autonomous decisions when adapting guidance from the task force. This could be done at the level of local subsidiaries, which had to integrate global corporate guidance with local regulation development, but also at the level of individual business units or functions. This became more important, the more global and diversified the organization (e.g. Novartis, Zurich, Zühlke).

Interestingly, several senior leaders pointed to the importance of not deciding too fast. Processes to seek feedback from peers, pause and make a choice after at least some reflection helped prevent speed spiraling into chaos. In the words of the chairman of Zühlke: "There is always enough time to pause and make a good decision, especially in a crisis."

Connectedness: Finally, connectedness was the third success factor. It concerns the cross-functional flow of information, ideas, and decisions across organizational silos. As discontinuous change requires holistic reactions that are coordinated across functions and geographies on multiple hierarchical levels, connectedness is absolutely necessary for a synchronized reaction.

Particularly at the onset of the crisis, lateral connections between the employees were crucially important to keep connectedness high. Companies built on their existing capabilities and infrastructure in order to achieve this. If the infrastructure was already migrated to the cloud, this provided easy scalability; in other cases, servers had to be extended in order to support peak loads of communication (Tchibo). Knowledge sharing sessions from teams who were used to working remotely aided colleagues who were faced with this situation for the first time. In the case of organizations with subsidiaries in China, learnings how the colleagues dealt with the new realities of Covid was helpful across organizational levels. Coordination calls within functions were substantially ramped up—for example, from once a month to twice a week at Novartis. Informal communication is crucially

> *important; thus, bespoke communication channels for informal communication such as Slack or WhatsApp (at Tchibo) were supported. Self-organized ways of keeping engagement high—for example, through virtual coffee breaks between colleagues—were shared as inspirational stories through internal social media platforms. And new challenges—for example, in relation to cyber security—had to be addressed in this new reality of remote collaboration.*

Through all of these measures, leaders exemplified how a crisis doesn't have to lead to "command and control" management but can instead become an opportunity to transition to more resonant leadership, which a focus on empathy, connectedness, and increasing speed by distributing ownership across the workforce.

> **Lesson Learned:**
> As a leader, showing your own vulnerability, sharing ownership and actively asking for support can foster the sense of connectedness in your organization and speed up effective problem-solving.

6.4 Leverage Failures to Grow Collaborations

> If you don't make mistakes, you are not working on hard enough problems. And that's a big mistake.—Frank Wilczek

Another focal challenge for managing the collaborative advantage through the quality of interactions in your organization is how to deal with negative interactions: conflict, mistakes, and failure. The most resonant groups we have seen embrace them. As the owner of one of the most successful restaurants in America always tells waiters on their first day on the job [16], "The one thing we know about today is that it is not going to go perfectly. I mean, it could, but odds are really, really high that it won't. So here is how we will know if you had a good day. If you ask for help ten times, then we'll know it was good. If you try to do it all alone….".

Some of the most successful organizations establish dedicated formats for these negative interactions. For example, at Pixar, in a format called

BrainTrust, all the negative feedback and critiques from the screening of a new movie or show are collected, Sseal teamsT conduct a so-called after-action review (AAR)—without the team leader, allowing for the candid sharing of feedback and criticism. You can conduct your own AARs like this: after important meetings or workshops, or at turning points in a project, have everyone involved fill out a form that asks the following questions:

1. What is the status of the meeting? (green, yellow, red)
2. What was the goal of this workshop/meeting, etc.?
3. What happened?
4. What went well/what worked?
5. What could be improved? How?
6. What are the next steps?

You thus ensure not only that people learn from the workshop, but that they are also able to comment, give new perspectives, and even suggest some approaches and solutions for problems that came up. With a tool like this, you are able to create that famous Google moment, where a "random" employee stumbles upon a problem and finds a way to solve it.

Other examples of embracing failures are the so-called famous "failure wall" or "failure prizes," various companies have established to celebrate failure—and the learning that comes from it. Being clear that failure is not sanctioned in your organization will help your team members to develop trusting bonds and a resonant collaboration signature.

> **Quick Win:**
> Create room for failure
>
> - Set up a format like BrainTrust to consolidate negative feedback and critiques in order to conduct a so-called after-action review without the team leader to discuss criticism
> - Use tools like Yammer or Teams to make people aware of topics other people work on and challenges they face, thus creating an opportunity for collaboration in finding a solution
> - Create evaluation forms to assess the progress, highlights, and lowlights of projects or meetings—so that future projects can benefit from this evaluation
> - Embrace failures by making them more visible (for example, with a "failure wall") or even rewarding them (for example, a prize for the failure of the month)

All of these examples point to a crucial insight as you strive to nurture the collaborative advantage in your organization: Awkward and painful interactions are as important to collaborative advantage as the positive ones.

So far, we have mostly looked at how collaborative advantage enables leaders to scale their business. However, the reverse is also true: As organizations scale up, coordination challenges can mount and pose a threat to the flexible leveraging of resources throughout the organization that is needed for rapid growth. We call this the scaling trap [17].

6.5 Balance Structure and Autonomy to Manage the Scaling Trap

When Max Orgeldinger kicked off the weekly TLGG Consulting all-hands meeting with a call for "radical change," the room went silent [18]. It was May 2020, and the announcement came as a surprise to the whole team of this Berlin-based management consultancy for digital business transformation. Though existential threats are not uncommon in a start-up's growth cycle, the company had been spoiled by success.

After spinning off from its larger corporate parent, TLGG had seen explosive growth led by Orgeldinger: in two years, the young unit had increased its revenues sixfold and doubled its workforce, while remaining cash-flow positive. This enormous success was due in part to the spirit, flexibility, and flat hierarchies of the start-up, which felt empowering for the first ten employees. But for the next thirty, these same start-up hallmarks increasingly proved costly and inefficient. Orgeldinger realized that—like many start-ups that grow out from a small team of dedicated pioneers—TLGG found itself in a scaling trap: It had to adapt its structures and processes to organizational growth while running the risk of losing its unique entrepreneurial culture. Having started as a two-man show, TLGG lacked the structure and governance necessary to run a mid-sized company with a growing number of employees and clients. Introducing such inner structure, however, presented another challenge for the young company: to do so while preserving an agile and dynamic spirit.

Confronted with the scaling trap, the organization had to navigate a series of problems. As more employees joined the company, the once-successful strategy of "everyone does everything" transformed into unclear responsibilities and confusion. Without explicitly assigned tasks, roles, and deliverables, coordination became increasingly difficult. Decision-making processes seemed endless and often resulted in unsatisfactory outcomes that were not supported by all employees. The lack of structure even jeopardized TLGG's long-term goals and direction. Employees started to feel disoriented, frustrated, and exhausted, which soon caused overall company success to drop.

"The increasing dissatisfaction in the teams, and specifically the resignation of several of our top talents within a very short timespan, made me realize that we cannot continue like this," Orgeldinger recalls. An organizational transformation was indispensable to stabilize the company and safeguard future growth.

To further complicate matters, the young company had just been through a comprehensive organizational change the year before. Change fatigue was still prevalent, and many employees were skeptical about the plans for an even bigger organizational transformation. In fact, given the family-like culture of the young start-up, not only did Orgeldinger's message take employees by surprise, but some even felt betrayed and left out of the decision process. Whatever the next steps would be, the utmost priority was to not lose the "collegial DNA" that had characterized TLGG from early on, and which represented a key foundation of its rapid growth.

After Orgeldinger's announcement in May 2020, intense discussions evolved about TLGG's path into the future. If the start-up wanted to keep up with its growth ambitions and realize its full potential, it had to carefully develop a new organizational design, considering its internal culture and DNA as well as its external image as a dynamic, agile start-up with solid customer relations and profound business development capabilities.

Max Orgeldinger and his colleagues had to understand how they could introduce a new organizational design that kept pace with the company's growth while upholding the start-up spirit and agility? How could they grow while escaping the scaling trap? A successful transformation could open many opportunities for TLGG, but a false step could trigger risks and setbacks. The young start-up was in a bind.

Orgeldinger decided to adopt a team-of-teams structure. His idea was to split the inflexible organization into smaller, decentralized, and independent teams forming business units, each with one lead. Those "Micro-Enterprises" should be allowed to make their own decisions in order to foster entrepreneurship, customer centricity, and employee impact, while still following an overarching TLGG vision (Fig. 6.3).

Overall Structure:

A central leadership team would be responsible for setting common P&L goals and coordinating the separate business units in charge of project work.

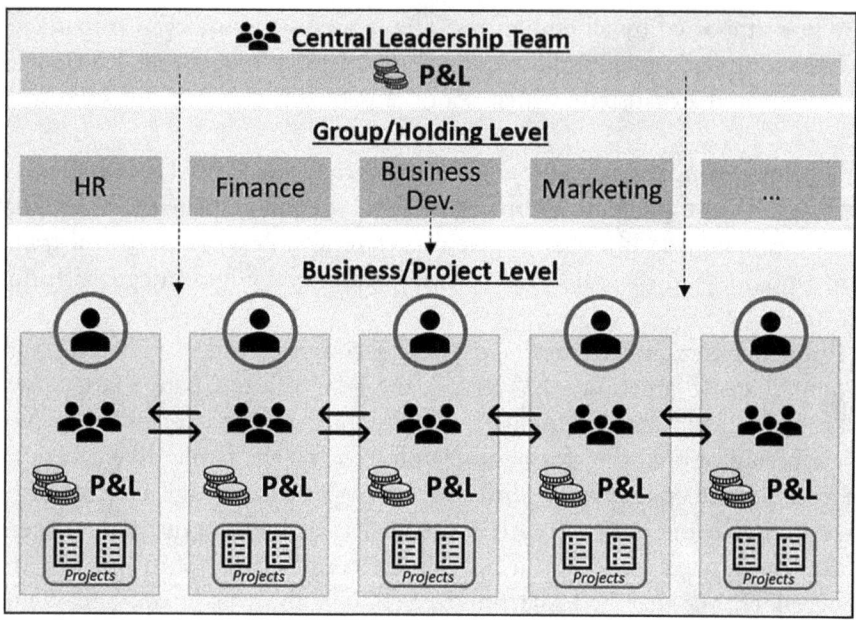

Fig. 6.3 Team of Teams at TLGG Consulting

These business units would consist of five to ten people each and a team lead elected by the team members. In addition to the overall goals, every business unit would be responsible for its own P&L target, the development of its team members, and its performance on projects. To achieve these goals, the individual business units would have full decision authority in terms of business strategy, employee management, and budgeting. As such, this team-of-teams logic wouldn't operate in terms of the usual profit–loss centers but would rather take the form of a marketplace with entrepreneurial freedom.

Roles and Characteristics:

In the team-of-teams logic, employees would be part of a fixed, self-selected team (business unit). They would have a constant team leader responsible for their work, performance, and personal development. In special cases—for instance, if a project could not be entirely staffed by the given business unit—another team would temporarily "lend out" some of its employees as support, getting a profit share in return.

Leadership positions would take the form of team leaders who would be appointed through a democratic election process. In their role, they would be responsible for a business unit of up to ten employees. They would be autonomous in making decisions for their respective business unit, but they would still have to ensure the achievement of certain common P&L goals.

Standard operational tasks, such as HR, finance, and marketing, would be bundled in a central administrative function, covering all business units.

For the development of new business opportunities, a "growth unit" would be formed, supporting team leaders in acquiring new customers and generating new project opportunities.

Through this change, the fledgling start-up was able to recapture the collaborative energy and speed of growth it had lost in its previous phase of expansion. Revenues consistently started growing again by over 30 percent per year, and the billability ratio improved by 50 percent, increasing profitability.

Through localizing collaborations and ownership, as well as creating mechanisms for synergies, TLGG was able to overcome the scaling trap and grow in a modular fashion that reduced complexity and thus coordination challenges.

> **Lesson Learned:**
> Organizational design can be an important factor fostering but also hindering effective collaboration—and can thus have a huge impact on your organization's performance and growth potential. It is therefore crucial to think carefully about an organizational design that fits your company culture, empowers your employees, and supports a collaboration network.

6.6 Three Take-Aways for Leaders

Leverage your ecosystem. Scaling is not only about growing; it is also about growing quickly and becoming more efficient while you're at it. Two main collaborative angles you can use to achieve this are (i) controlling coordination costs as much as possible while growing, and (ii) leveraging resources outside your formal zone of control.

> **Quick Win:**
> Reduce internal complexity by localizing everyday collaboration as much as feasible. Position underused experts, support overloaded bottlenecks, and scale up learning across your unit as quickly as possible. Externally, create win–win scenarios with external partners by aligning incentives and sharing complementary resources.

Make it resonate. A resonating collaboration signature is a focal predictor of group excellence in scaling up. This is driven by two processes: Social learning of best practices and "tricks of the trade," and social energizing to tap the discretional energy of your employees.

> **Quick Win:**
> Look for the following indicators in your organization: Close physical proximity, profuse amounts of eye contact, physical touching, lots of short energetic exchanges rather than long speeches, high levels of mixing and spontaneous interactions, few interruptions, lots of questions, active listening, shared sense of humor, small courtesies to each other.

I'm all about that nudge. In order to nudge the collaborative advantage in your organization toward a more resonating one, think about nudges that influence the quantity of interactions and nudges that influence the quality of interactions.

> **Quick Win:**
> Don't get cute: Relatively simple nudges can yield disproportional results. It's not about finding innovative ways to create collaboration, it is about understanding what kind of collaboration to create and where precisely to create it.

6.7 Ideas for Action: Simple Practices

Get a wingman. Alternately assign your product-development teams as wingmen to each other. For example, at Pivotal, a cloud-based software company, developers work in pairs during new product development. They share their screens, ideas, and even meals. This intense experience of collaboration allows them to simulate the Pink Panther effect. We recommend switching up these pairs at least every two quarters in order to keep the flow of ideas and insights fresh.

Experience purpose. As we have seen in the case of the fundraising call center, direct experiences of how their work has impacted actual human beings is a huge driver of relational energy. For example, a Swiss telco company capitalized on customers who indicated high satisfaction with their service in a survey and had employees from non-customer-facing departments call these customers and thank them for their feedback and loyalty. This provided a huge engagement boost for employees in these departments and sparked a variety of improvement projects based on the interactions.

Signing off bonus. Take a page out of Valve's playbook and offer new hires a signing off bonus, if they feel like the job is not a good cultural fit after the initial training period. We know from research that only a few "rotten apples" can undermine relational energy and thus performance—even in larger groups. Make sure people who are excited to share and collaborate are not pulled down by colleagues with a much more transactional mindset.

Collaboration as career. Provide recognition and rewards for the kind of peer support behind a resonant collaborative advantage. For example, at Google, employees even in non-leadership roles are evaluated based on the criterion "makes their colleagues more effective." A bit more systemically, we have seen organizations track Net Promoter Scores for internal service providers in order to drive colleague-centricity and collaboration levels comparable to those in customer-facing roles.

6.8 Ideas for Action: Advanced Practices

Merging departments. Follow innovation leaders such as Lego and Dyson, and organize teams along collaborative rather than functional lines. For example, revenue teams that are segmented along typical customer journeys rather than arbitrary hand-offs between marketing and sales provide a much more complete and integrated experience not only to potential customers, but also to employees working with them. Other examples include D4B teams (Lego) or design engineering units (Dyson).

De-Bottlenecking. A major threat to the efficiency of such collaborative models are bottlenecks. Technical experts and middle managers can quickly become overloaded and put the brakes on other teams as they wait for decisions, resources, or critical insights. Regularly collecting data on this, such as in the Halliburton case, as well as leadership coaching can provide a way forward.

Early Ownership. Instead of always going to the same five people for critical projects, distribute ownership for important work earlier and more broadly. For example, at PWC, so-called squads tasked with improving work in an agile way have been recruited by squad leaders based on decentral signing-on bonuses.

6.9 Collaborative Scaling in Action at Amazon

Few companies embody aggressive scaling and hypergrowth as much as Amazon. At the same time, the company is widely seen as efficient and frugal. How does Amazon manage its hypergrowth without leaving their culture and efficiency behind?

Back in 2002, a request made by book publisher Tim O'Reilly inspired the development of Amazon's uniquely scalable way of growing revolutionary new lines of business, such as Amazon Web Services (AWS), Fulfilment By Amazon (FBA), and Amazon Alexa. O'Reilly asked for a way to make sales data from the Amazon Marketplace available to third parties, allowing them to track trends, supporting publishing decisions. He suggested implementing online tools, so-called application programming interfaces (APIs), enabling other websites to build on Amazon's data. When Bezos first questioned how this added value for Amazon, O'Reilly pointed out that "companies need to think not just what they can get for themselves from new technologies but how they can enable others."

With this statement, O'Reilly convinced Bezos of the enormous potential behind APIs, not only for Amazon's external web presence but also for its internal processes, leading to the following mandates:

- *All teams will henceforth expose their data and functionality through service interfaces.*
- *Teams must communicate with each other through these interfaces.*
- *There will be no other form of inter-process communication allowed: no direct linking, no direct reads of another team's data store, no shared-memory model, no back-doors whatsoever. The only communication allowed is via service interface calls over the network.*
- *It doesn't matter what technology they use. HTTP, Corba, Pubsub, custom protocols—doesn't matter.*
- *All service interfaces, without exception, must be designed from the ground up to be externalizable. That is to say, the team must plan and design to be able to expose the interface to developers in the outside world. No exceptions.*
    via https://gist.github.com/chitchcock/1281611, Stevey Yegge, former Amazon employee

These guidelines not only affected the development of software within Amazon but revolutionized internal collaboration. Instead of closed communication from desk to desk, employees were asked to use APIs to communicate, creating a more open exchange between Amazon's teams, organized by division. As the company scaled up, this reduced the added coordination cost of onboarding unfamiliar teams and introducing them to the right experts. Instead, by accessing the scalable structure of APIs, new units could quickly and efficiently leverage resources and insights throughout the company. For instance, if earlier, one product team requested statistics from another group via email, they now hit the product team's API to access the data directly. Any of the many divisionally organized teams decoupled their resources, embracing accessibility and making those resources available for the whole organization via an API in a design that could always be sold to third parties. Such service-oriented architecture caused each team to operate as a self-contained service unit and transformed Amazon culturally into a service-centered organization. This way, Amazon not only promoted? internal services but also reduced the need for inefficient redundant communication and embraced a healthy platform mindset.

> "We expected all the teams internally from that point on to build in a decoupled, API-access fashion, and then all of the internal teams inside of Amazon expected to be able to consume their peer internal development team services in that way. So very quietly around 2000, we became a services company with really no fanfare."
> Andy Jassy, AWS CEO

Consider what this means for the ability to rapidly scale up promising new ventures through seamless access to resources such as data and technical infrastructure within the company. A policy of complete accessibility and availability sent a strong message to employees about how to collaborate. Indeed, Bezos had an exceptional take on communication within his company. In the early years of Amazon, when the company was starting to grow meaning he coordination of teams and divisions became more complex, Bezos argued that "communication is a sign of dysfunction. It means people aren't working together in a close, organic way. We should be trying to figure out a way for teams to communicate less with each other, not more."

This mirrors the lessons on the scaling trap we discussed above: For Bezos, creating teams with limited communication but an organic way of interaction turned out to be very useful. First, through internal API service channels, disrupting requests and one-way information exchange between teams became obsolete. Second, creating smaller units reduced the amount of communication necessary to implement useful and intuitive habits, enhancing collaboration.

Aiming to achieve a decentralized organization in early 2002, Bezos implemented today's famous "two-pizza rule." Amazon organized employees into autonomous groups covering all functions needed for their specific task but still small enough to be fed with two pizzas. This allowed the company to implement a fast-moving and agile working environment. It seems teams of four to ten people was the perfect size for maintaining a structure of sorts while creating an environment for natural autonomous human communication without many hierarchy levels. With the goal of becoming one of the most innovative companies in world history, Amazon recognized very early that "a hierarchy is not responsive enough to change" and implemented an organizational structure enabling fast and independent decision-making.

> *We have the good fortune of a large, inventive team and a patient, pioneering, customer-obsessed culture – great innovations, large and small, are happening every day on behalf of customers, and at all levels throughout the company. This decentralized distribution of invention throughout the company – not limited to the company's senior leaders – is the only way to get robust, high-throughput innovation.*
> *Shareholder Letter 2014*

A well-functioning and, at the same time, innovative enterprise requires the best of both worlds. While scale, financial resources, and global scope make you robust, the entrepreneurial spirit remains essential to innovation. Consider Bezos's notion of the "Day One" mentality:

> *"Day 2 is stasis. Followed by irrelevance. Followed by excruciating, painful decline. Followed by death. And that is why it is always Day 1." Bezos*

While retaining a start-up spirit even after 25 years in business might seem like an impossible challenge, Amazon established several practices to support its Day 1 drive in an efficient and scalable way. Consider these four principles: First, being customer-obsessed ensures a strict focus and a clear mission. Second, results being more important than processes give flexibility and autonomy, allowing you to organize your team according to intuitive working habits. Third, few hierarchical levels and small groups enable fast decision-making with efficient communication. Fourth, keeping an eye on environment and external changes, ideas, and trends can be a source of great innovation.

The only fixed rule at Amazon for how to access resources and scale up centers on how new ideas should be put forward. The so-called "Working Backward Process" is a standard interface for putting ideas into play, starting with a description of the desired outcome from a customer perspective. It should yield a six-page description of the concept. One page must consist of a press release. It should explain the underlying problem, who benefits in what way, and how the product will look. It should include FAQs and a level of detail that would satisfy a future customer. Finally, the working backward process includes a portrayal of customer experiences in the form of a prototype or a mock-up.

The tool was designed to allow effective communication without losing focus through misleading PowerPoint presentations—and to force people to dig deep into the ideas they were proposing. It is meant to empower any employee to bring up an idea no matter their function. Such a document can be presented to anyone who can allocate resources. Doing so fosters ownership and engagement, and it invites anyone to think big and outside one's box.

6.9.1 Collaborative Analytics at Amazon

In addition to taking these technical and cultural approaches to scaling up innovation, Amazon also incorporated data driven decision-making that enabled it to quickly outperform competitors. Naturally, this also extended to how collaborative advantage is managed at the group.

Amazon's growth ventures are very much dependent on boundary-spanning collaboration. Practices such as the Working Backwards process or Think Big conferences are meant to engender this type of collaboration. At the same time, broad collaboration brings about the danger of collaborative overload, and may position managers as bottlenecks.

This danger was tackled at Amazon Devices with a collaboration analytics project. A look at the data helped identify overloaded employees, who were tapped too often for approvals or access to technical resources. These insights helped the team to alleviate cross-team dependencies, reduce the need for approvals, and provide better access to technical resources in a hyper-targeted manner. These goals were achieved with measures such as combining some teams under common leaders for faster decision-making, making other teams smaller, spreading collaborative work more broadly, and establishing processes for central employees to monitor and manage their collaborative loads.

In addition, collaboration analytics were used at a department- and team-level to find quicker ways to onboard people into collaborative work, better connect isolated or peripheral units, and better spread work fairly. These broader insights helped Amazon make better and more targeted decisions. For example, they used the data to (1) prioritize teams with stagnant networks and low collaborative workloads for coaching and critical path work; (2) identify teams where workloads and relational access were imbalanced, supplying tools and training for information sharing; (3) locate teams that were running hot with collaborative demands and complex or shifting networks, and decelerate demands as much as possible to reduce risk of burnout; and (4) illuminate teams with positive external interactions with customers, in order to ensure the glow of customer-focused transformation reached every employee.

These types of analysis showcase the potential for using data-driven decision-making to empower an organization—to not only creatively spot emerging opportunities, but also to execute these opportunities with overflowing energy and uncompromising speed.

6.9.2 Scaling Up Infrastructure on Demand/ Infrastructure as a Service

From Day One, Jeff Bezos believed in Amazon's future as a technology enterprise rather than a simple eCommerce reseller. As such, he encouraged people to explore opportunities outside of Amazon's core business. Emerging from this encouragement, Amazon established "Look/Search inside the book," paving the way for the modern e-book business.

Especially when exploring new, unfamiliar sectors, many companies struggle with the institutional "no," meaning any sign of internal resistance to the unknown. Bezos didn't want his companies creating this effect. As he put it, talking about the need to be a technology company: "There's only one way out of this predicament, and that is to invent our way out."

In terms of that economy of internal APIs, it soon became apparent that such a service-oriented architecture (SOA) enabled the design of platforms. Translating their own need for a service into building scalable applications for the broader market, Amazon has pursued its ambition for API networks under the name Amazon Web Services. Afraid of guessing attractive services based on habits of the past, the company chose the concept of primitives, the smallest possible computing element, to break Amazon's infrastructure down into its very essential parts. Emerging from several brainstorming sessions with the goal of stimulating creativity among AWS developers, a set of primitives were derived. Teams of developers were then formed to build services covering the defined primitives such as storage, computing, database, messaging, bandwidth, and payment. Allowed unlimited flexibility, the teams were free to decide on their organization and their working habits.

One team lead by Chris Pinkham, a former head of IT infrastructure, even decided to leave Amazon's headquarter in Seattle to work in isolation in a newly opened office in Cape Town on a service that allowed third parties to run applications on Amazon's servers. Building on open-source codes, his team managed to develop a service called Elastic Compute Cloud (EC2), laying the foundation for today's modern cloud economy. In the past, Amazon started experimenting with external development centers, cut loose from ongoing activities in its headquarters. Such remote satellite locations enabled the group to enter areas with rich pools of technical talent. While making use of established networks and collaborative advantage, it allowed the harnessing of new energy and creating an agile start-up spirit within these satellite offices. While reducing the need for complex communication and coordination efforts via decentralization, the offices remained connected via regular update meetings. The very first external development center, A9, was dedicated to exploring ambitious ideas outside of Amazon's core business, such as the search engine business. Followed by further locations such as Lab126, Amazon explored ambitions in consumer electronics that led to innovations including the Kindle, Fire Phone, and Amazon Echo.

At the same time, another team consisting of twelve engineers basically lived together and grew close during the following two years to build the service Simple Storage Service (S3). They even had their own T(eam)-Shirt with an adapted version of Superman the S—but theirs was S3.

The very first web service, "Mechanical Turk," a crowdsourcing platform for low-wage jobs, later turned out to be a source of innovation. Developed as an internal API, Mechanical Turk allowed for the coordination of smaller tasks such as reviewing Search Inside the Book scans and product images uploaded by marketplace resellers. After successful internal implementation, Mechanical Turk launched in 2005 for the external market, allowing companies to make use of Amazon's API to list jobs and access the global on-demand workforce. The platform is still online today, though lagging far behind Bezos's expectations in terms of user numbers and financial results. Building on experiences from Mechanical Turk, Amazon developed further seminal web services rooted in internal needs. Within months of each other, S3 and the EC2 launched to external customers, jointly transforming entire industries.

> **Lesson Learned:**
>
> What can we learn from Amazon's aggressive scaling and hypergrowth?
> Amazon's success story can be viewed as an interplay of various measures that optimized its collaboration signature—for example:
>
> - Creating an open exchange between Amazon's divisionally organized teams to quickly and efficiently leverage resources and insights throughout the company

- Setting up teams with limited communication but with an organic way of interacting by organizing employees in autonomous groups covering all functions needed for their specific task, but limited to four to ten persons per team
- Being customer-obsessed
- Focusing on results before processes
- Having few hierarchical levels and small groups for fast decision-making
- Keeping an eye on its environment and external changes, ideas, and trends
- Allowing experimentation with ideas and helping employees think their ideas through effectively
- Being extremely disciplined in quickly and ruthlessly killing off innovations that don't perform, to make room for new ones.
- Enabling data-driven decision-making based on collaborative analytics

Invention comes in many forms and at many scales. The most radical and transformative of inventions are often those that empower others to unleash their creativity – to pursue their dreams.
Shareholder Letter 2011

6.10 The Next Step

If you want to turbocharge collaborative scaling for your organization, go to collaborative-advantage.org/scaling for suggestions and resources on how to get started. Among other offerings, you will find:

- A one-hour sample workshop for discussing the potential of collaborative scaling and potential action items with your relevant stakeholders (complete with agenda, pre-reads, suggested slides, and outcomes)
- A video with a senior leader's personal reflections on collaborative scaling

You can also scan the QR Code if you don't like typing. The resources are all free.

References

In order to keep the book lean enough to comfortably be read on a plane, we have listed the full references on the companion website for your convenience. If you want to dig deeper, please check them out here:

10. Collaborative-advantage.org/references-scaling/10.
11. Collaborative-advantage.org/references-scaling/11.
12. Collaborative-advantage.org/references-scaling/12.
13. Collaborative-advantage.org/references-scaling/13.
14. Collaborative-advantage.org/references-scaling/14.
15. Collaborative-advantage.org/references-scaling/15.
16. Collaborative-advantage.org/references-scaling/16.
17. Collaborative-advantage.org/references-scaling/17.
18. Collaborative-advantage.org/references-scaling/18.

Part IV

Collaborative Transformation

7

Overcoming Corporate Silos

> *The nation will find it very hard to look up to the leaders who are keeping their ears to the ground.*
> —Sir Winston Churchill

7.1 Disrupt Rigid Collaborations to Increase Openness to Change

When Kun-Hee took over as President and CEO of Samsung Electronics, he found himself in a situation in which the company was doing well and, in a culture, where respect for the elder or the senior was one of the cornerstones. This entrenched a company DNA at Samsung where tradition was central. But the visionary Kun-Hee Lee saw the need to change: He knew that Samsung needed to become a much more adaptive organization to survive in the twenty first century. But how to change a culture completely when there was seemingly no urgent pressure to do so? As a young man, he had watched closely and learned during his father's tenure. He had kept a low profile when first at the helm himself, but knew which direction he wanted to take. He even did something that was then, and still, is very uncommon within Korean culture: he went against his father's judgment to invest (personally) in the semi-conductor business. Would he be able to do something just as radical with his company, bringing it into the twenty first century?

When it came to achieve his ambitious goal, Kun-Hee Lee focused on renewing the competitiveness and adaptability of Samsung as whole [1]. He called this the New Management Initiative. Under this mundane label he had hidden a revolutionary ambition: He would go on to completely challenge his father's fast-follower strategy and catch up with the international players through investing in research and technology. He thus changed the whole logic of the organization into first/mover thinking. But only investing in R&D was not enough. He also had to have a closer look at how the DNA of the company was to be transformed.

For chairman Lee, his view in the rearview mirror highlighted dangers to the competitiveness of Samsung that might resonate with executives from many large companies we have worked with over the years. The size of the group had developed into a protective cushion that effectively uncoupled large parts of the organization from external market pressures. The majority of the units were focused on servicing internal customers who were flush with cash and mostly obliged to source products and services from these internal vendors. Even customer-facing elements of the organization were to some degree shielded from market pressures: The size of Samsung translated into huge economies of scale, which helped to deflate costs and thus reduced the pressure to compete and innovate as hard as smaller competitors had to. Taken together, the internal prospects of the group's business units were far too dependent on their ability to navigate internal politics and negotiate access to Samsung's vast resource base and too little dependent on their performance in the marketplace.

This dynamic also had implications for the corporate culture. A rigid and exclusive focus on the shared identity of belonging to Samsung had developed. This tribal culture led to an internal protectionism forced by social pressure, where uncompetitive affiliates and initiatives were underwritten by more successful ones—a dynamic students of Japanese *keiretsu* have described as "quiet life equilibrium." For Lee, these trends were alarming as they would erode the competitiveness of Samsung and replace bold strategic vision with managerial navel-gazing and defensiveness. His concerns would be proven right with the onset of the Asian financial crisis, which resulted in massive losses and impending failures at Samsung.

The New Management Initiative was his recipe for transforming Samsung into a top-tier company. His vision: Instead of one colossus suffering enormous inertia and misaligned incentives, he would develop Samsung into a network of more nimble, semi-independent units. Influenced by an American mindset, Lee wanted to move toward an individual-driven company. The self-viable units he would free from the lumbering giant were to compete much more autonomously, each as their own profit center, in order to align incentives: profit-sharing schemes raised the stakes for leaders and employees to collaborate to make *their* units successful; at the same time, units that didn't turn a profit for three years in a row were to be discontinued or restructured (excluding new business, for which tailored goals were negotiated with the group management). This scheme was substantial and extended through the entire hierarchy of each unit, thus creating a set of shared and localized incentives. Meanwhile, salaries, bonuses, and promotions were to be based on absolute evaluation (achievement of goals) and relative evaluation (compared with affiliates, divisions, teams, and individuals). For example, the annual base salary of employees depended on the performance of the business units they belonged to and the results of their relative performance appraisal. Therefore, employees of high-performing business units had a much higher annual salary than those from low-performing business units (up to one and a half times larger). This led to vehement negotiations in internal transactions, but also to tight emergent cooperation among business units when the cooperation was mutually beneficial.

Kickstarting this vision required some real creativity: As the new approach disrupted the sheltering economies of scale that units at Samsung had profited from, competitive advantage had to be developed through product quality and innovation instead of merely through low internal costs. When some units didn't shift gears fast enough, Lee frustratedly assembled more than 2000 employees at the Koomi factory near Taegu, which had a high deficiency rate. He wanted to make a clear statement. A statement no employee would forget. A statement through which employees understood how seriously he was when he said he wanted them to point out errors to their bosses, and that quality always goes over quantity. At his signal, members of his staff started breaking down boxes full of freshly made cellular phones, key phones, and facsimiles amounting to 150,000 sets worth about 1.5 billion won. The broken sets were ceremoniously burned in the yard of the factory, while Lee addressed the crowd: "Let us never make a single defective product even at the cost of our production lines being shut down." Understandably, this rather drastic experience left an impression on the management team.

The new vision of a network of autonomous units also meant much more freedom in managing the relationships between these units into one of cooperation. Two cornerstone policies of Lee's initiative illustrate how this worked in practice.

First, remember that one of the problems he diagnosed lay in sheltered and uncompetitive internal vendors. To tackle this, he instituted the policy of *dual sourcing*. This meant that internal and external vendors would compete on equal footing in terms of quality, prices, and delivery times. Each unit would have the flexibility to source the products and services they needed to conduct their business wherever they wanted—without any need to justify their decisions, other than with a strong P&L. In the words of Lee: "Whether we provide or purchase a service or product, we must create a level playing field of competition for affiliates and outside businesses. In this way, only capable firms can partner with us, enhancing our own competitiveness. This will truly create synergy for the group as a whole." For the first time, this exposed internal vendors to a direct market environment instead of one governed by internal politics. For example, Samsung Electronics' mobile phone division procured mobile application processors solely from Qualcomm, although Samsung Electronics System LSI division also produced the processors. The mobile phone division had drastically reduced procurement of the processors from the System LSI Division as the latter had difficulty in developing high-end mobile application processors. At the same time, the policy opened up huge and lucrative external market opportunities... if the unit would be able to seize them. For market-facing vendors, dual sourcing increased their exposure to diverse potential suppliers and partners, each with their own unique technology stack and capability base. These would serve as important impulses for employees to more quickly sense and seize shifts in technologies and customer demands.

Second, for strategically important developments, Samsung would engage in *parallel development*. This meant contracting multiple units at the same time to deliver a product and then choosing the most competitive one. While this carries the danger of wasting resources through redundant efforts, if too prevalent, it can create real options and unlock a focused energy for important sprints when done strategically. It gives the company room to break free from the path dependencies of their past practices and adopt changes through a survival-of-the-fittest competition. In this way, parallel development presents an internal Darwinian selection mechanism to experiment with different technology stacks. At the same time, the extraordinarily high compensation Samsung awarded to high-performing divisions gave this internal contest real teeth. To see the policy in practice, consider the development of organic LED display technology at Samsung (OLED): From 2004 to 2008, two major Samsung affiliates competed vigorously to develop the OLED technology more quickly and better than the other. Consequently, the two affiliates alternately grabbed "world's first" titles for technology development and market releases. Between 2001 and 2010, the OLED R&D team at Samsung Electronics' LCD division registered 776 U.S. patents related to OLED technology, while its counterpart at Samsung SDI registered 755 U.S. patents. As the need for large-scale production grew in 2008, Samsung decided to merge Samsung SDI's and Samsung Electronics' OLED teams to form Samsung Mobile Display. The new company dominated the OLED market thanks to product technologies from Samsung SDI and manufacturing expertise from Samsung Electronics' LCD division. Under the coordination scheme of group headquarters, the two Samsung affiliates have cooperated with each other by moving their key engineers to Samsung Mobile Display.

An important piece of the parallel development policy happens directly after such internal competitions end: Several joint, cooperative initiatives in win–win scenarios follow, both to avoid the festering of any conflicts, and to exchange learnings throughout the competition, and diversify the knowledge base throughout the organization.

Lee made sure in other ways, too, to drive cooperation alongside competition. Through targeted formats such as in-house technology forums and conferences, data sharing, and rotations of key personnel across the units, Samsung ensured both formal and informal interfaces through which knowledge and resources could flow across unit boundaries. Returning to the case of OLED displays, we can illustrate the internal cooperation that takes place alongside internal competition. Here, Samsung Display closely collaborated with Samsung Electronic's mobile phone division to develop OLED display panels that could fit in the smartphone. Since there was only one supplier of the panels in the world at the time, the demand for panels vastly exceeded supply. Samsung Display was able to provide almost 90 percent of its output to Samsung Electronics' mobile phone division, allowing Samsung smartphones to secure a competitive advantage in image quality. Likewise, Samsung's mobile phone division also helped Samsung Display develop key technologies to reduce air gaps between liquid–crystal display and touch screen panels so that it could make its smartphone thinner, and optimize battery life. Additionally, the mobile phone division shared its product roadmap with Samsung Display so that Samsung Display could develop panels for the division faster than could outside vendors. Most importantly, Samsung Electronics' mobile phone division, the world's top producer of smartphones, provided Samsung's semi-conductor division and Samsung Display with a stable source of demand.

Importantly, these practices are energized by the intensive local and unit-based incentive scheme outlined above. Specifically, people are highly motivated to achieve the best quality possible and to bring their departments to another level because their salaries, and the very existence of their departments, are directly coupled with the department's success and the employee's contribution to it.

Becoming this network of largely autonomous units made Samsung as a whole much more adaptable. On the one hand, the requirement for each unit to be "self-viable" led to an organic, constantly ongoing restructuring where the company divested irrelevant or uncompetitive capabilities and invested in emerging opportunities. On the other hand, the open internal competition created the necessary urgency to innovate—a notoriously difficult challenge in large companies. For example, when Samsung Electronics eliminated Samsung Electro-Mechanics from bidding for the supply of electrolytic condensers, this came as a huge shock to the unit. This shock, however, created the necessary impetus for Samsung Electro-Mechanics to improve the quality of its high value-added products such as multi-layer ceramic condensers to world-class levels.

> **Lesson Learned:**
> Most transformations are managed with a focus on individual employees (convincing, upskilling, enabling). But the success of transformations is more dependent on relations (coalitions, adversaries, networks, peer pressure) than on the opinions of individual employees.
> These are typically measured and managed much less professionally (or even less consciously) than individual employees.

Through his New Management Initiative, Lee had helped Samsung renew its capabilities and transform into a highly adaptive and competitive organization. This strategic re-positioning paid huge dividends when a disruptive innovation shattered one of Samsung's most important markets: The advent of the smartphone. In order to appreciate the strategic context in which Samsung found itself quite suddenly, we have to contrast the reaction of Samsung with those of other companies similarly affected. When Steve Jobs introduced the iPhone, the implications famously blindsided many companies. Steve Ballmer, then-CEO of Microsoft, missed the opportunity to enter an emerging market Microsoft might have seemed destined to win, while struggling analogue photography companies such as Kodak were wiped out. But no firm epitomizes the failure to adapt to the smartphone revolution quite so much as Nokia.

Samsung was, from the perspective of their offering, in a very similar position to Nokia: A successful and important player in the feature-phone market without a market position for the smartphone age. Unlike Nokia, however, it had gone through the extensive internal renewal process under the New Management Initiative. When the iPhone was introduced, this allowed Samsung to innovate at breakneck speed: A network of some of the most successful units formed in order to develop their own Smartphone, the Galaxy S1. Only *six months* after they started development, their product was successfully launched. Three years later, Samsung had overtaken Apple and dominated the Smartphone market with more than 31 percent market share compared to Apple's 15 percent (measured by units sold), a position they continue to hold to this day (or at least as of the writing of this book).

Samsung succeeded in its transformation because it disrupted both overly formalized and rigid internal collaboration structures and increased the surface of the organization exposed to external coopetition by breaking up the lumbering giant into a network of much smaller, more autonomous units.

This approach, which highlights the importance of collaboration, has been behind some of the most successful transformations. Consider the turnaround of Disney Animations under Ed Catmull, or the successful repositioning of Springer after being disrupted by free online journalism. In each of these cases, acquisitions brought in new coalitions to shake up rigid structures. In addition, leaders transformed the way employees collaborated, creating collisions between diverse perspectives and energizing a movement for renewal.

Instead of classical change management, the collaborative approach acknowledges that companies rarely successfully transform on their own. Rather, this approach opens up the organization through acqui-hires in order to bring new talent into the leadership pools, uses partnerships and rotations to bring in new perspectives, and leverages acquisitions to build positions and capabilities in growth markets.

Quick Win:
A change in collaboration structures can be a key ingredient for a successful transformation. This can be achieved by...

- Breaking up a rigid and inflexible organization into smaller, autonomous, and more agile units
- Introducing profit-sharing schemes with performance-based components in these local, autonomous units
- Fostering collaboration between these new units (knowledge exchanges, data sharing, personnel rotations), while at the same time creating a sense of competition

- Energizing initial change through culturally appropriate, creative leadership approaches (such as the public burning of deficient manufactured goods in the case of Samsung)
- Launching internal competition sprints between units to turbocharge crucial initiatives (such as parallel development, again in the case of Samsung)

7.2 Apply Leadership Rotations to Foster a Unified Vision

How do you transform a declining former colony without any natural resources into one of the most productive, prosperous, and innovative economies in the world? When Singapore became independent from Malaysia, it didn't look poised to become a success story. In fact, its GDP per capita was a mere $516, half the population was illiterate, and a third of its people squatted in slums on city fringes. Fast forward to today, and the country has the second-highest per capita GDP in the world (at purchasing power parity) and was rated in 2019 as the most open economy by the World Economic Forum, the third least corrupt, and with the highest amount of economic freedom [2].

Lee Kuan Yew, Goh Keng Swee, and the other early leaders of the new state had the advantage that they could build on deep personal connections, formed during their shared time as students in the UK in the 1940s. They were certainly aware that transforming Singapore into a prosperous city-state and providing financial security to its people was a daunting task. Just take a moment to imagine the sense of scope and responsibility as they set out to design a competitive economy based on not much more than pure chutzpah. And imagine how empowering the sense of sworn community among the senior officials was for them, as they built on deep connections and a shared sense of purpose to tackle this defining challenge of their lifetimes.

The leaders of this nascent state quickly agreed on their working hypothesis—how they could go about realizing their vision of a thriving economy: Build an environment completely aligned on the goal of supreme business confidence in order to attract major investments from international companies. But how could they transform an entire nation in order to make Singapore attractive to foreign executives? They focused on two central priorities: Creating a completely non-corrupt government, and radically changing their citizens' behavior to create a pristine physical environment. Just how smart and relevant these goals were would later be highlighted by CEOs talking about their decisions to set up in Singapore: "There was absolutely no corruption and they kept their promises." The spotless new airport was likened by visitors to Zurich (incidentally another country whose wealth is mostly built on supreme business confidence).

But successful transformation is not only about a sagely strategic vision—it is really about execution, and about how the myriad daily choices of individual people can be transformed in a coordinated way to build an organization with innovative new capabilities. In order to execute on their vision, Singapore's leaders created a bespoke network: The economic development board (EDB), a quasi-governmental organization staffed with some of the country's best executives, such as Philip Yeo, who became its first chief executive.

How the unique and often unconventional management practices of the EDB made the transformation of Singapore possible can best be understood from a collaborative advantage perspective: Everyone in the government had multiple jobs, and relational cohesion was crucial—built around the shared purpose of transforming Singapore's economy. This required everyone to foster a high degree of openness, trust, and collaboration. The EDB achieved this by having senior leaders rotate their areas of responsibility. In this way, everyone was familiar with all elements of government. Tribal thinking in terms of maximizing the performance of your particular fiefdom was replaced with an expansive experience of group accountability for the entire organization. Even though units and leaders in other contexts would compete with one another, this rotation approach was crucial to developing mutual cooperation *concurrently*. Reminiscent of Samsung's transformation, no? Wherein a collaboration signature characterized by simultaneous cooperation and competition played a crucial role in transforming an organization. We will return to this observation in more detail in the next chapter. For now, let's stick with Singapore's economic miracle.

Another management challenge from a collaborative advantage perspective—one we have touched upon a few times now—is combining internal cohesiveness and resonance with external openness and the break-up of echo chambers. How was this challenge dealt with by the EDB? The answer is in its personnel policy.

Lee Kuan Yew had recruited the best and brightest young Singaporeans to staff his nascent government. He gave them scholarships to go to the best western universities, and then brought them back for five years of service in government at competitive pay levels. This ensured that he could attract and retain the best—a difficult challenge when recruiting for public sector jobs.

But his investment in developing high-potentials and then providing opportunities comparable to elite private sector careers paid off. It also ensured that people independently formed their own perceptions and created their own learnings and networks.

Most managers might have observed the incredible internal collaborative advantage the setting of the EDB was almost certain to create, and would have run with it: A sworn community of the best and brightest working day and night intensely together on the hardest and most important challenge of their lives? This is a perfect recipe for an intensely resonant collaboration signature. But Lee knew that, in order to be sustainably successful, he would have to complement this cohesiveness with the openness. He would have to invite in external perspectives, build relationships, and become a central hub in a global network of excellence. Consider how his policies came together to achieve this: New staff would not only bring their own global networks from their government-funded scholarships at top universities; they would also mostly leave for the private sector after five years. This inherent churn ensures fresh perspectives, as well as creating a web of deep personal connections bridging fault lines between the government and the private sector through the alumni who would go on to staff elite private organizations.

> **Self-Reflection:**
> How do you keep up with employees who leave the company? Do you leverage them as trusted brokers to provide you access to knowledge and opportunities from other organizations?

7.3 Use Collaborative Incentives to Energize Transformation

This motif is also apparent in the further development of the EDB. Over the course of Singapore's transformation, the EDB became an international organization with officers placed in essentially all the major industrial centers. The goal was both to learn from the private sector and to develop personal relations with executives that might result in investment in Singapore. This strategy paid off: Foreign executives were consistently impressed with the technical knowledge, education, and interpersonal abilities of the EBD officers.

Lee also highlighted the importance of social learning and external openness in the senior leadership. In designing and implementing his policies he sought the help of the United Nations and various European advisers with comparable experiences of building a young country. He also made sure to have the government learn from industry as the first multinationals began to set up in Singapore. For example, he took personnel administration manuals from Royal Dutch Shell, a company he admired.

And how about the internal collaboration signature in the young government? We already pointed to the rotation practice at the senior leadership level that broke up siloed thinking. How did Lee ensure boundary-spanning, flexible collaboration down the hierarchy? He first made sure that officers in the EDB had both the license and the mandate to talk to anyone up or down the hierarchy if it concerned present or future investors. No rank or protocol could stand in the way or override bringing the right people together to pursue an investment opportunity.

The value he placed on collaboration extended to incentives. For example, promotions were clearly based on a combination of individual talent and demonstrated ability to collaborate with others. Frequent job rotations made it possible to get to know everyone in the organization, such that trust and openness could be maintained. In interviews, young EDB officers explained that they were in competition with each other for promotions but that the ability to flexibly form and work in teams was one of the main criteria on which they were competitively evaluated.

We can also see the philosophy behind Singapore's success in the leadership style of the senior officers. Philip Yeo, the former head of the EDB, highlighted how his bias for action translated into how he worked with his subordinates. Rather than asking, "why should we do this?" he would ask "why *not*?" His colleagues described his leadership style as follows: "To get the best out of people, don't be paternalistic. You have to treat them like kites… You get them up in the air, if there's no wind, you try again. Everybody needs a lift off. If they get into trouble, you reel them in". Yeo credited his ability to let his followers "fly like kites" with his own deeply resonant relationship with his own boss, Goh, who detested micro-management and supported Yeo's entrepreneurial risk-taking.

Quick Win:
Measures to improve the collaboration signature in your company:

- Encourage job rotations, including of senior leadership, to avoid siloed thinking and protectionism
- Feature collaboration as part of the promotion requirements, for example by including criteria such as "makes their colleagues more effective"
- Foster entrepreneurial experiments by challenging yourself to ask "why not?" instead of "why?"

The successful transformation of Singapore's economy to a thriving city-state was enabled by the collaborative advantage of its EDB, purposefully designed and managed by its senior leaders. Its management practices were designed to attract the best and produce a collaboration signature that was both deeply resonant internally and diverse and open externally. Boundary-spanning collaboration was enabled with relational incentives and practices designed to circumvent bottlenecks and leadership support. Finally, many direct interfaces with a core constituency of foreign executives created client relationships on which to base investments.

Highlighting the success of Singapore as a case for collaborative advantage might seem odd given some of its less liberal policies. For example, changing citizenship behavior and cleaning up the city was at times enforced with rather draconian laws. However, this critique is based on confusion around the point of collaborative advantage. Collaborative advantage doesn't mean "being nice" or ignoring transactional incentives in favor of a community feeling. Fundamentally, collaborative advantage means acknowledging the primacy of peer relationships in motivating, energizing, and guiding behavior and performance. Managing it requires a psychologically literate reading of the relational architecture in an organization in order to change collaborative signatures to energize and align the behavior and performance of the organizational members.

In this sense, collaborative advantage is a perspective that provides actionable angles to transform the way groups behave and perform, in light of your goals. Does the economic success of Singapore and the delivery of opportunities and security to its citizens justify the hard decisions that got them there? This is a personal value judgment everyone must make for themselves. Collaborative advantage, as we have tried to describe it, is a fungible tool to achieve goals independent of their moral worth.

Most readers, we expect, however, will have more humble aspirations than transforming an entire economy. Can leaders capitalize on collaborative advantage and deploy similar principles to those we described in the Singapore case in order to transform their organizations? Let's consider the case of the Virginia Mason Medical Center (VM) in Seattle.

7.4 Build on Joint Field Trips to Align Departments Behind Transformation

When Gary Kaplan took office as the new CEO at VM after twenty years under his predecessor, the organization was facing challenging times. The group's financial performance was bad, and there was a looming conflict between the culture and political interests of the administrative staff and the medical staff. Kaplan was an MD whose specialty was internal medicine, and he lacked much formal education in management. He was, however, renowned as a forward thinker who could take an expansive perspective and focus on the hospital's improvement rather than the self-interest of particular coalitions.

Under the headline of "the new compact," he immediately started working on what we would call the collaborative advantage of the organization [3]. He knew that incessant infighting would stop any serious attempt at transformation unless he could unite the staff into a cohesive, energized, and adaptive team through a new relational contract. What did every group and coalition owe the others? What values and perspectives were shared among them to serve as a basis for cooperation and synergies—and which aspects were unique, and could serve as complements and inspiration?

Kaplan conducted a series of relational workshops. Leaders from both the medical and administrative communities co-developed a shared purpose around improving patient safety and experience. This purpose would serve as the bedrock on which the new compact would be built—and it would outline each group's responsibilities for moving the organization toward this purpose. Simply put, the new compact served as a value declaration of the shared identity of the different communities making up the hospital. Helped by this shared starting point, everyone began to realize that they needed to collaborate across their respective silos. Kaplan required all parties to live by the new compact. If they couldn't do it alone, they should get coaching. And if they didn't want that, they should leave.

Still, while the compact was a strong cornerstone, it remained abstract and aspirational: To translate it into the lived experience of VM, it would have to be executed on. Kaplan organized retreats with several hundred key doctors and administrators to help them develop personal, informal relationships and explore common ground. These relationships would later prove the basis for the personal trust and shared commitment necessary to energize the coming transformation.

After creating and shaping his coalition of senior leaders, Kaplan focused on finding a common framework of reference for managing the transformation. As is so often the case, he eventually found inspiration far outside his typical peer group: Carolyn Corvi, a senior executive at Boeing, inspired him when she described to him her experience of implementing the lean methodology in her company. Even more serendipitously, another VM executive met a consultant on a flight who would come to provide invaluable expertise and guidance in VM's lean roll-out. To Kaplan, this proved a great fit for his challenge. Through teaching everybody in the change program the same methodology, a common frame of reference and shared language would align the various implementation initiatives throughout the organization.

A central challenge for any transformation is ensuring enthusiastic, sustainable commitment for the process in the upper echelons of the organization. Kaplan was unusually successful in aligning his leadership team behind the transformation through the clever use of collaborative advantage: In order to directly experience the benefits of the new system *in a relational way* and learn together as a team about it, he took a number of key physician-leaders, administrators, and board members on a 14-day study trip to Japan. Here, the leaders could learn firsthand and together how the Toyota production system had been implemented in different industries. After the trip, the entire group made the decision together to go forward with the new methodology at VM. In fact, Kaplan became so convinced of the importance of this trip that he made annual trips to Japan to learn about making lean implementation a standing policy at VM. In his own words: "It is not enough for the board members to *understand* the program and to *bless* it, because they will not really understand what is involved personally in some of these transformational changes that the doctors and administrators will have to go through unless they have themselves had a personal learning experience which gave them not just insight but active enthusiasm for what was going on." Besides this energizing effect, he also noted side effects on the collaboration signature in his senior leadership team: "By going on these trips and learning together, they formed relationships that made the board useful as an essential support system." In fact, today all board members must participate in this two-week learning experience in Japan some time within their first three-year term in order to be eligible for reappointment.

This leads to another observation: Transformation projects are often canceled even if they are successful—for example, if the board doesn't understand the scope and scale of the transformation process, and brings in a new CEO. The deep relational contract shared by the entire senior leadership (both management and board) that Kaplan has developed through his

Japanese excursions is what keeps the transformation alive and successful at VM.

> **Quick Win:**
> Field trips to best-in-class role models can align senior leadership behind your vision for the transformation.

The relational perspective behind the transformation of VM is also apparent in the implementation of lean into the processes. Cross-functional teams throughout VM learned about lean in workshop experiences. Volunteer teams then began to collaborate in improvement events to re-design their processes. An extended group of stakeholders of employees of all levels and functions as well as patients and their families served as a sounding board to guide and steer the improvements to solutions that actually worked in their own lived practice.

> **Lesson Learned:**
> Achieving collaborative advantage in your organization often starts with a collaborative approach. This can involve relational workshops with leaders from different departments to develop a shared purpose. This purpose can be brought to life in field trips, where your staff can build up interpersonal relations; and the collaborative signature can be kept alive through ongoing personal learning experiences.

At VM, the new relational compact between stakeholders was also key in negotiating the implications of the change: After all, in Kaplan's first workshops, the groups had aligned behind the shared purpose of improving total patient experience. This was a big change; the system at VM had been designed to provide *the best experience for the doctors*. Take, as an example, the cancer center. Before, patients had to run all over the hospital to get diagnosed and receive treatment; they had to re-introduce their data and needs to changing staff at each station. Under the new compact, the team wanted to bring all diagnostic equipment and therapeutic processes into the same area. However, this was not feasible in the former cancer center. Instead, they would need to get the dermatology department to give up their space.

VM wasn't the only hospital with problems like these. If you've ever visited an emergency room, you'll note that, as much as patients there are often in extreme pain, they will not normally see a doctor directly. First comes patient administration, with questions and form-filling—and an opportunity to explain why you're there. Unfortunately, this story will have to be told, on average, another three to four times before receiving treatment—to a nurse doing triage, perhaps to another nurse assigned your case in particular, to a medical student or assistant, to a resident physician, and perhaps finally to a senior physician. This is a tiring and often frustrating process for patients, and gives the impression that no one working in the hospital talks to one another at all.

A possible solution is to have a highly skilled person at the beginning of the process in order to precisely triage the patient and give them the care they need. This might seem counterintuitive; a highly skilled physician should focus on the severe cases, not see everyone who walks through the doors. But that doctor's experience means they will be able to identify in no-time what kind of care each patient needs, and they will know who to call. Mistakes are less likely to be made on the triage decision. With this change in the process, it is also possible to release "minor cases" immediately after entering the ER, keeping the whole waiting room from being filled with those cases, and making more time for the patients who need more care. But back to VM:

In most organizations we have studied, the cancer center vs dermatology department would be a tough test: Who has access to which offices, who gets new facilities, whose teams are together versus spread all around the organizational campus… setting aside compensation, few topics inflame managerial egos more. In Kaplan's estimation, he could not have succeeded in convincing the dermatology department to give up their space for the good of the organization without his deep investments in building trust, shared purpose, collective ownership, and mutual commitment throughout the transformation—or, in other words, his management of collaborative advantage.

Through this collaborative transformation, VM was able to implement many changes to improve patient experience and safety and thus differentiate itself as a high-quality care provider. For example, the emergency room was able to sharply reduce waiting times and patient discomfort; wait time came down through co-location of critical functions, and wards were redesigned to facilitate nursing–patient interactions instead of shielding nurses from patients in their stations. Also, a version of the famous Toyota practice of stopping the production line was implemented: If any member of the treatment group perceived a problem, they could immediately stop the treatment process and gather all relevant team leaders and their leaders to get a prompt review. This also stimulated closer relationships across the medical hierarchy continuum. And another Toyota practice came into play—Kaizen. Kaizen is Japanese for "good change" or continuous improvement. What is interesting here is that every professional group, regardless of whether it is composed of doctors, nurses, physiotherapists, or nursing assistants, can make suggestions for improvement. Problems are identified and solutions put forward, and once a week, or bi-weekly, all the ideas are discussed, and the status quo challenged. Each new idea is categorized: is it something that should be implemented immediately? Is consultation needed? Should it be kept in mind for later? And every idea has a person responsible for it, is assigned measurements for how to quantify success, and is given a testing and implementation date. The meetings are in part there to see whether that responsible person or team needs support or input from someone else.

> **Quick Win:**
> Try the Kaizen approach:
>
> - Everyone in your organization can make a proposal for an improvement (including the explanation of the underlying problem and ideas for a solution, its implementation, and success measurement), thereby assume ownership for this specific idea
> - All ideas for improvement are collected and then discussed in a weekly or bi-weekly meeting to decide which ones should be implemented directly, which ones should be kept for later, and which ones are not of interest at the moment
> - Also, use these meetings to identify the need for support in order to realize an idea

Through smartly managing the collaborative advantage, Kaplan was able to fundamentally and successfully transform VM from a declining, technocratic organization plagued by infighting and silo thinking to an "example of what is possible" (Kenny 2011; Plsek 2014) in the medical sector. He created a new relational contract between the different coalitions based on collective accountability for patient safety and experience, heavily invested in joint, direct and relational learning through field trips with established and emerging leaders, and finally rolled out local adaptive changes through empowered, energized local teams.

7.5 Use Local Empowerment to Transform Your Organizations into a Leader-Leader System

> Leadership and learning are indispensable to each other.—John F. Kennedy

We have discussed both the transformation of Singapore and of VM with a focus on the collaboration signatures of senior leadership teams. This is both because these collaboration signatures are the necessary basis for transforming organizations, and also because we expect most readers to be interested in how they might apply collaborative advantage principles within their direct sphere of influence—their peer group.

But strong early signals within the senior leadership can also propagate down the hierarchy and encompass an entire organization. This requires ruthless consistency and commitment. Take the case of the transformation of a demoralized, low-performing U.S. Navy nuclear submarine into one of the highest-performing units in the fleet [4].

The transformation took place under one Captain Marquet. In describing his approach, he explains his ambition was to transform his ship from a *leader–follower system* into a *leader-leader system*. Instead of having his people passively await orders and avoid errors, he wanted them to take initiative and seek out excellence. So when he started inviting initiatives from his leadership team to adapt and transform the organization, it took tremendous consistency to nudge rather than command his employees out of their comfortable, passive roles. He writes about his approach: "Like so many times, my not knowing the answer ahead of time helped me. Instead of a scripted meeting where I pretended to solicit ideas, we had an honest conversation."

> **Self-Reflection:**
>
> Think about the meeting structure in your organization: do you have a scripted agenda with all the solutions already in your mind? Or do meetings resemble more of an honest conversation with everyone bringing in their ideas?

The first idea brought to Marquet wasn't really what he had been hoping for: His chief council suggested they streamline vacation policy. Per Navy regulations, any leave of absence had to be approved by all seven levels of the ship's hierarchy. Naturally, this made vacation planning very difficult for many sailors. However, Marquet decided to go out on a limb and make a judgment call to break Navy regulations on his ship, switching to requiring only that a person's immediate supervisor approve leave requests. He later reflected that this decision was hugely important in kickstarting the entire transformation that followed. He set an example, taking a substantial personal risk in overriding regulations and traditions to empower local flexibility. After all, if an accident had occurred and an investigation found that he had breached protocol in the run-up to it, there was a real chance he would have lost his position and his accrued pension entitlements. His crew started to realize that he was all-in for finding new ways of doing things, that he was willing to put himself on the line and try unconventional approaches. Most importantly, he was willing to find ways to meet their personal needs rather than narrowly focusing on performance standards. Not surprisingly, the new system was an immediate morale booster and invited many more empowered local improvement initiatives. It transformed the collaborative advantage between commanding officers, NCOs, and sailors—from hierarchical toward a partnership of attentive and sovereign humans united by shared goals.

> **Quick Win:**
> Create buy-in for your transformation by making early interactions beneficial to others. Start by providing value, before asking for engagement.

Through a consistent policy of radical openness and fixing problems rather than assigning blame, Marquet's approach to transformation propagated down the hierarchy. As the officers found it easier to exercise their own judgment in their areas of expertise and to make flexible decisions, they also found it easier to also pass the same power down to their own direct reports. In turn, as local ownership increased, the staff spotted ever more potential for improvement and took the initiative in adapting their local sphere of control.

The transformation of the submarine illustrates another core principle of collaborative advantage for transformation: The collaboration signature you as a leader design between you and your direct reports scales down to how they will relate to their own direct reports. In this way, taking the principles shown in the first two cases in order to nurture collaborative advantage for transformation within your own senior leadership council has profound implications for how they will in turn manage the collaborative advantage within their own spheres of influence.

> **Lesson Learned:**
> A successful transformation starts by setting an example as a leader. You need to show full commitment to your employees and "act the change" rather than just "talk the change." Meeting their needs may involve taking risks sometimes, but it will create a collaborative atmosphere that will boost their motivation.

7.6 Employ Collaborative Incentives to Drive Behavior Change More Effectively

> Effective leadership is not about making speeches; it is defined by results, not attributes.—Peter Drucker

We have observed how relational interventions and management of the collaboration signature have energized strategic vision into successful transformation. But in order to apply these principles to your own practice, let's quickly take a step back and look at them more systematically.

> **Self-Reflection:**
> Imagine the following situation:
> You are approached by a nervous operative from a federal intelligence service. He proceeds to explain that he needs your help in finding ten red balloons that contain critical information as soon as possible. The problem is that these balloons could be anywhere in the United States. How would you go about trying to find these balloons? And what is your estimate of how long it would take you?

This is the basic setting of a challenge given from the Defense Advanced Research Projects Agency, or DARPA. As the U.S. government agency tasked with developing emerging technologies for military use, it is increasingly responsible for "inventing the future" in the US.

In the aforementioned challenge, the agency was interested in creative ways of organizing the sort of instant collaboration that might be required for disaster relief. An expert interviewed described the challenge as "impossible to solve by conventional intelligence-gathering methods." And yet, a team of researchers from MIT managed to identify the correct GPS coordinates for all balloons in under nine hours. They achieved this through the clever use of collaborative advantage [5].

The researchers decided to tackle the challenge by creating an instant organization of volunteers spanning span the entire US to look for the balloons. But while most teams in the competition tried to do this by offering individuals money for finding balloons, the research team devised an incentive plan that capitalized on the power of collaborative advantage. They understood that, rationally, nobody had a particularly strong incentive to change their behavior and look for red balloons on their behalf. After all, it is incredibly unlikely you would be the particular person to find the balloon. But they also understood that relational motivations are much stronger than these rational considerations.

As we have discussed, collaborative advantage can energize your employees to do their jobs and execute at a transformative level. This relational motivation is also a key part of using collaborative advantage for transformation. But instead of using collaborative advantage to energize employees to do more effectively what they have already been doing, this time we want to employ it to energize them to change. In order to explain what the researcher group did and why it worked, let's look at some basic principles of how to use relational motivation to drive behavior *change*:

At congressional mid-term elections in the US, voter turnout is invariably fairly low. The reasons are familiar to most transformation managers: Voting is uncomfortable, a change of routine bothersome, and the benefits are more systemic than personal. In order to get people to break out of their routines and vote, something has to energize them. A project from Facebook and researchers from the University of California at San Diego strived to assess the potential for personal relationships to serve as this energizing function.

In order to document the importance of relationships for voting behavior, the researchers compared two simple interventions: One group of voters received a simple "get out and vote" message. The other group received the same message, but with an additional detail: They also saw the faces of their friends who had already voted.

Based on an analysis of 61 million Facebook users, the difference was transformative [6]: While there was a slight effect from the simple "get out and vote" message, it didn't really move the needle in terms of voting behavior. However, the group that saw the faces of their friends who had already voted showed a substantial increase in voting behavior. Intrigued, the researchers further analyzed the second group, and found that the increased voting was almost exclusively driven by a single effect: The number of close friends to which they already had a face-to-face relationship among the faces of voters Facebook showed them. In fact, these close friends had more than four times as much as influence on the voting behavior as the message itself. Through making the voting behavior of close friends highly visible, each individual vote generated on average three other votes through this engineered social contagion.

The results reinforce the importance of close relationships for energizing uncomfortable behavior. This is in line with the difference between the collaboration signature that brings new ideas into the organization (connections with diverse, otherwise not connected tribes) and the collaboration signature that drives execution (collaborative connections within tribes of similar people). Similar to the more tacit knowledge and complex motivations behind the collaboration signature for seizing opportunities, relational drivers of change are mostly based on close and similar peers.

From an evolutionary background, this makes perfect sense: If there is a new trend occurring within your tribe, it is hugely adaptive to be on top of this trend in order to not be left behind, losing your social status. In fact, during Raphael's tim at the Social Psychology Department at Stanford, we routinely used this insight in our work. For social experiments, it was often imperative to engineer certain attitude- and behavior changes in participants in order to isolate their causal role in the study outcomes. One of the more successful ways to do this was to frame target attitudes as rising trends among the relevant social reference group of the participant. Marketing to customers often intuitively applies this insight: It is all about you and your people, and how the product enriches your daily life. Unfortunately, much internal communication in transformation programs is really the opposite.

Of course, the "get out and vote" project has some limitations in how generalizable it is to organizational transformation. Most importantly, it was focused on getting individuals to change their routine for one specific action. In contrast, most transformation initiatives have the added hurdle of having to maintain change. Can collaborative advantage also help to engender sustainable change? It can. Let's look at two examples of notoriously difficult-to-maintain changes.

The first project was aimed at increasing levels of physical exercise among Bostonians. As anyone who ever had the misfortune to spend a winter in Boston will readily admit, the weather is not the sort to lure you outside. Predictably, this leads many Bostonians to decrease their level of physical activity over the cold months. Even more problematically, these reduced activity levels are often sticky long into the summer. Low levels of physical activity are associated with all kinds of societal costs, such as obesity, diabetes, and depression.

In comparison to the "get out and vote" project, this was a much harder problem to solve since it required consistent, effortful behavior change on the part of the participants. In addition, it wasn't as simple to show close peers exercising: Because activity levels were so low to begin with, the entire change had to be both kickstarted and made sustainable.

The solution turned out to be simple and ingenious: Relational incentives for close groups of peers, or "buddies" [7]. Using relational analytics, buddy groups were identified. These consisted of about three individuals who interacted *regularly* and *positively* with each other. Now, instead of incentivizing individuals based on their own behavior change, as in a classical, individualized approach, the participants were incentivized based on the behavior change of the other members of their buddy group. Each individual got small cash *incentives based on improvements in physical activity of their close peers.*

In effect, this turns around the incentive for behavior change from an individual one to a relational one: I don't change for my own, relatively marginal benefit. But I do change in accordance with the social expectations of my close peers. In order to evaluate the relative effectiveness of this approach, physical activity was collected using smartphone data. Instead of an artificial experimental set-up, the changes had to work and stick out in the real world, with all its distractions and complications.

In the end, the relational incentive turned out to be four times more effective in promoting behavior change than traditional, individually focused approaches. For buddies who had the most interactions with each other, the relational approach was eight times better than a standard approach. In other words, the same number of resources invested in relational incentives yielded a substantially larger change effect than if it were invested in classical, individual incentives. Even more importantly, the behavior change based on relational incentives was *sustainable even after the incentives were discontinued*.

The second example, completed in cooperation between Oliver's institute and MIT, tackles a challenge that combines problems from both examples [8]. In addition, it shows how cleverly designed relational incentives can still be effective even without a complete relational analysis.

The project, which was completed in Switzerland, was focused on reducing the energy consumption of local residents. Similar to the "get out and vote" project, it was targeting uncomfortable behavior change with mostly systemic benefits for everyone, rather than individual benefits. Similar to the Boston exercise project, it required a sustainable change in behavior.

In the first phase of the project, the energy consumption of residents in the target canton was analyzed. Those residents then received an analysis of their consumption compared to average consumption. However, there were two different versions of this report: In the standard version, the resident's consumption was compared with consumption by all other people in the country. This approach was wholly ineffective and resulted in virtual no behavior change. In the second version, the resident's consumption was compared with that of his or her close reference group—in this case, the neighbors. This worked significantly better, resulting in modest behavior changes.

Again, these first results shouldn't be too surprising to you as the reader: After all, we have repeatedly seen the primacy of close, local relations for behavior change as compared to broader social groups. Based on these insights, our group designed relational incentives similarly to the Boston physical exercise project. Participants were invited to form voluntary buddy groups with their friends and were rewarded not based on their own behavior change, but on the changes of their buddies.

The relational incentives again proved transformative, resulting in energy consumption reduction *at twice the rate of the best reduction campaigns documented before* and more than four times the rate of the average campaign. Again, the results also document the primacy of the relational part of the incentive over the financial incentive: On average, participants received a financial incentive of a measly 50 cents per week. For comparison, energy price elasticity curves suggest that in order to achieve the same reduction in consumption based on financial incentives, energy prices would have to *double*.

> **Quick Win:**
>
> Think about the four use cases of collaboration analytics to empower your transformation:
>
> - Prioritize: Understand the impact of ongoing transformation activities on everyday behavior and prioritize activities that move the needle.
> - Optimize: Make transformation activities more impactful, for example by specifically identifying, onboarding, and empowering hidden influencers as transformation champions.
> - Nudge: Nudge behaviors in line with the transformation vision by strategically building work interfaces between successful role models and slow adopters.
> - Feedback: Provide regular, timely, and visual feedback to employees to capitalize on their self-regulation toward behaviors in line with the transformation vision.

What makes relational incentives so effective and sustainable in motivating change? We have repeatedly discussed the importance of close social peers for energizing behavior. Relational incentives tap into this energy and use it to motivate change. In the "get out and vote" project, this was done by showing that close peers already show the targeted change. That is, they vote In both the exercise project and the energy project, the change was motivated by making the behavior change an investment in the relationship. It is not about the objective results; it is about socially signaling to people who are important to you that they matter to you and they benefit from your work. This relational motivation is much more important than the objective payout, which makes it possible to use comparatively tiny incentives to affect huge, transformative change.

The anchoring in close peer groups also explains the sustainability of relational incentive-induced changes. Individual incentives often get some people in a group to change, but not others. As soon as the external incentive and persuasion stop, the psychological force field will again be dominated by close peers. Through conformity pressures, this will lead the individual to abandon their changed behavior. A typical example of this in the corporate context are change workshops, which get participants temporally excited about new perspectives. As soon as they return to their old environment, the peer pressures in these environments revert them to their old mindsets and behaviors. In contrast, relational incentives influence close peer groups together, making the change work with the conformity pressure instead of against it. Similar patterns of social voting between peers have also been observed in primates, which voice their preferences, for example, through head movements in rapid cycles of recruitment and expression until a tipping point has been reached: Then, a consensus is established and everyone falls in line and adopts the consensus as a guide for their own behavior.

Maybe you have heard the adage that in all your attitudes and characteristics, you are the average of the six people you spend the most time with? Social engagement and pressures of conformity and cohesion within the collaboration signature between close peers are the driving forces behind this observation.

Let's now test these dynamics and their applicability to change in the organizational setting. Consider a project aimed at understanding to what degree a collaboration signature governs the adoption of new digital tools in organizations. This analysis was based on the introduction of corporate social media platforms in more than 1000 companies and millions of interactions behind them.

Acceptance and sustainable usage of the new tool was governed by the same relational principles we have documented above. Critical for the adoption of the change were bursts of relational recommendations, a rush toward the new behavior. Again, this is similar to the trend logic described above. If anyone received three or more recommendations for using the new tool in a short time frame from close peers with pre-existing relationships, the employee was all but guaranteed to join in. In contrast, even 12 recommendations from more distant colleagues only had a very small effect on technology adoption within the same time frame. In an organizational setting, too, then, a change of habits requires several examples of trusted peers successfully using or recommending the new behavior [9].

> **Lesson Learned:**
> The importance of relational incentives:
>   Close relationships with peers are crucial for energizing new and uncomfortable behaviors sustainably. While people are often resistant to change individually, they are very willing to engage in change in accordance with the social expectations of their close peers. Thus, incentivizing your employees based on the changes in behavior of their other team members will motivate them in adapting a new behavior, as they perceive it as an investment into their relationships with their "work buddies." Additionally, as relational incentives influence close peer groups as one, changes will be made with the conformity pressure, not against it.

Armed with this new understanding of the collaboration signature behind change, let us return to our hapless intelligence officer and the challenge of the ten lost red balloons. From a collaboration signature point of view, the challenge to motivate people you have never met to look for balloons is all about behavior change. And as we have learned, this is guided by the process of engagement, which is powered by social interactions with close, personal contacts. In order to tap into this process, the researchers changed the incentive from individual to relational. In their plan, not only would the person who found a balloon be rewarded, but also the person who recruited the finder, as well as the person who recruited the recruiter, and so on (Fig. 7.1):

This relational incentive fundamentally changed the motivation from an individual-rational one (I want to make money) to a relational one (I want to demonstrate to my friends that I am a good and loyal friend). In postmortem interviews, participants said they would recruit their friends because it was "like sending them a free lottery ticket." Searching for balloons did not only become an activity to benefit oneself, but a social signal to the close peer group which guides behavior. In other words, they changed the incentive from one aimed at individuals to one aimed at relations.

In the end, the army of volunteers consisted of almost two million people. Based on this instant organization, they were able to achieve a feat deemed all but impossible by experts in the field in little more than a working day. The researchers achieved this extraordinary feat by creatively capitalizing on collaborative advantage.

> **Quick Win:**
> - Incentivize behavioral changes based on team and peer behavior, rather than purely on individual behavior.

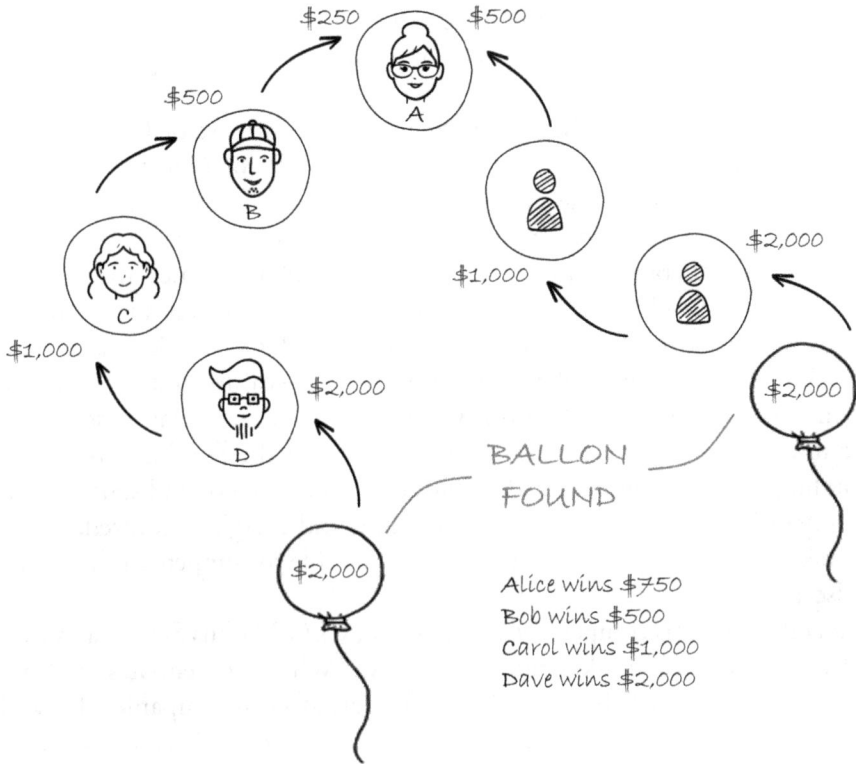

Fig. 7.1 Incentive scheme of the red balloon challenge

> • Grow communities around important transformation topics by asking participants to sign up their friends and colleagues.

7.7 Spark a Movement Behind Your Transformation by Connecting Change-Agents

Let us look at how these collaborative advantage principles come together in the transformation of a large public chemical company: Covestro. For Covestro, the need and mandate to transform came directly with its birth: When its parent company, the pharma group Bayer, announced that they would spin-off and IPO their material science division, this required the new entity, called Covestro, to develop its own unique identity. As a manager of the company told us in an interview: "You were told that you were outside alone now. No longer in this Bayer Group. You have to exist apart. That did unsettle many."

The challenge of transforming their identity from part of big corporate group to a new distinct player came at a time of major industry upheaval, moreover. Traditionally, the chemicals industry was based on long-lasting, personal relationships between suppliers, producers, and clients. Producers such as Bayer generally sold close to 90 percent of their products directly and in large volumes. However, emerging trends of digitalization and customer centricity started to change this landscape. New digital marketplaces were emerging which followed platform logics. As is typical for industries which become transformed into platform systems, many different players started to race toward positioning themselves as the owner of the dominant platform, including chemical companies, distributors, online retailers, and start-ups. As their traditional products were commoditized and margins squeezed, Covestro needed to quickly transform in order to be able to compete in the digital landscape.

In addressing this competitive requirement, CEO Markus Steilemann gave a clear mandate to think unconventionally. "What differentiates us from BASF (...), a GE or a Sabik? In the end, these are all great companies. They all have super products, super technology, and smart people. (...) What differentiates [Covestro] are the people, the culture, the understanding: Do they want and like to work here? And do they know why they work here?".

Inspiring... but he met substantial challenges. For example, in order to find new ways to compete, everyone had to be involved in innovation. Finding new and better ways to service customers, innovating along the supply chain, and developing adaptive digital processes required an all-in approach. Consequently, innovation needed to be defined broadly. Jens Joschek, who led the innovation excellence program for the transformation, recalls: "The difference to Bayer is that now all are innovators. We all listen; all are bright minds. On different levels and that is okay too. Not everyone has to invent the billion-dollar business."

But this clashed with the old idea from Bayer that innovation was "what happened in the R&D department." Nor was R&D happy about this change, as they had vested their identity in the organization in being "the" innovators. But this was also why Jens Joschek was so important for the transformation. He is the type of person who likes to challenge the status quo and doesn't back down from challenges—even when success requires enormous time talking to people intensely and persuading them of your cause. Joschek told us the new expansive understanding of innovation necessitated a broad mandate to innovate: "And R&D cannot do that. R&D is a function that has an important role, but (…) they can only make products, they cannot make business models, they cannot innovate processes."

When exploring the issue, Joschek knew he had to find a way to get R&D on board, and needed to respond to their needs. He recognized he could address the issue by finding new ways to celebrate and highlight their valuable contributions. Soon a Science Award, a Science Medal, and a Tech Day were being developed and rolled out, all with the goal of recognizing outstanding inventions.

If you take a step back, both the challenge and the solution are easy to understand from a relational perspective: As a new transformed logic of innovation started to emerge, it threatened the social recognition and social identity of the crucial tribe of R&D scientists. It challenged what made them unique. But by finding ways to present them and their work as still unique and valuable, both a cohesive sense of identity within the tribe and relational recognition from the broader company could be reinstated. Thus, the R&D department was brought back into the fold—which is to say, buy-in for the transformation program.

In addition, for the transformation to work, hierarchical processes needed to change. Instead of command-and-control, fast local decision-making by empowered networks of local experts spanning functional boundaries needed to be developed in order to truly transform Covestro into a digitally innovative player. This challenge was highlighted by employees' transformation fatigue; they had, after all, just emerged from an extensive reorganization after the carve-out.

In mastering these challenges, the transformation team at Covestro applied many of the collaborative advantage principles we have discussed. Take the importance of peer influence for behavior change, as demonstrated in the platform introduction study above. After launching their Start-Up Challenge, the innovation excellence team heavily invested in providing the innovation champions a platform to distribute their influence in their local network. Marc Schreiber, a winner of the Start-Up Challenge, told us: "I do not think that there is anything more credible for the innovation process than colleagues telling their colleagues that it is possible. When innovation managers tell us how innovative we are and what great things we do, I do not think it works." Similar to what the research tells us, in the case of Covestro, behavior change was all about the opinions and influence of colleagues who are similar to you—not about the opinions of senior leaders.

> **Quick Win:**
> Energize your transformation by identifying, enrolling, and aligning key opinion leaders.

This philosophy also heavily influenced the innovation excellence (IE) team's battle for the hearts and minds of the employees. They were uncompromisingly focused on creating and empowering local, self-organizing communities that could build cohesion and collaborate around the topic of innovation. Rebecca Heil, from the IE team, told us: "Since we said, somehow, we cannot push the button and bring out a new IT tool (…) [we] needed people, ambassadors. And that is where we started to build up a group that also functions as network nodes within the company—for example, through a network called tIdea.Pilot Community." This philosophy was further highlighted by Jensch Joschek, the head of the IE team: "We did not send anything centrally. Of course, we gave them material. But they planned events with their budget. I would say there it starts with the culture—if they take it for themselves and not 'we are in this because the CEO wants it'. Instead, it adds value for us, as an initiative."

Alongside the Idea.Dot Community (consisting of roughly 300 people with people intrinsically motivated around the topic of innovation), the IE team also created Idea.Pilot (a group of sixty people worldwide ready to give valuable feedback to the IE team). Covestro created platforms (Idea.Lab, Inno.Talks, Start-up Challenge, etc.) to establish and nourishing environments and increase the quantity of interactions. This also helped to break down silos by encouraging employees to leave their echo chambers and discuss their ideas with peers from other departments or even form new and more diverse group to generate ideas, or to serve as ambassadors to transform their local work communities.

As highlighted in our discussion of Singapore, relational transformation doesn't only just transforming lateral connections across silos; it also means transforming vertical, hierarchical relationships. Here, too, the IE team served as a crucial. As Joschek told us: "We were simply well networked, and we also had the standing that when we delivered something, it had relevance, and it was needed. (…). We opened many doors to top management and said: 'Why do you not go and talk to him?'".

To make this work, they needed to empower local decision-making. Senior vice president Hermann Bach explained this philosophy: "We are driving the idea that we have 17,000 employees. And we want to be able to rightly claim that this means we have 17,000 innovators. So, you can be just as innovative in HR as in the laboratory—as with business models or as in production—when it comes to how we can further reduce our costs and better utilize our facilities."

In addition, relational transformations are often enabled by open external interfaces from the company to bring in external ideas and resources, create lived experience of change and thus highlight the urgency to adapt. Thus, as part of their transformation, the company opened up and invested heavily into their organization-spanning networks, collaborating with research institutions and bringing in external partners such as suppliers, customers, and consultants to help them guide the change. All of this was built on a foundation of enabling relational tribes to transform their local spheres of influence and improve, adapt, and evolve. Again, Joschek: "We innovate to generate better, faster, and stronger volume more profitably. We are not innovating because we have a KPI of twelve new patents in half a year or so. That is not the driver. And that is a little rethinking from processes to content. Also, that is why it is so much about communication, a lot about leadership, […] and that plays into the culture again. What offers can the organization give the employees to make this rethinking easier?".

> **Lesson Learned:**
> Key success drivers of transformations:
>
> - Beware of the social recognition and social identity of your individual teams in your organization, as a transformation may challenge what makes them unique. Finding new ways to value their work is crucial for transformational success
> - Avoid command-and-control for the benefit of fast local decision-making by empowered networks of experts and self-organizing communities
> - Provide the innovation champions a platform to distribute their influence in their local network and share their knowledge
> - Foster behavior change through the opinions and influence of colleagues who are similar—and not just through the opinions of senior leaders
> - Create platforms to increase the quantity of interactions and break down silos by encouraging employees to leave their echo chambers and discuss their ideas with different peers
> - Transform not only lateral connections across silos but also vertical, hierarchical relationships. For example, designate brokers who can put employees with good ideas in front of relevant decision-makers
> - Enable open interfaces to bring in external ideas and resources and foster collaboration with external partners to challenge current ways of working

Through this transformation, the company has transformed its DNA. It is now a holistic innovation builder with an energized network of 17,000 innovators. The company's start-up program was awarded the prestigious best innovation culture award from the ZEIT newspaper. And they have already started establishing themselves as a leading digital player—for example, with the newly launched, in-house-developed digital trading platform Asellion.

7.8 Assemble a Diverse Coalition to Increase Adaptability

> A leader is a dealer in hope.—Napoleon Bonaparte

So far, we have established how the intelligent use of collaborative advantage can help engender both large and lasting changes in attitudes and behavior. This is a crucial element of many organizational transformations. On the other hand, organizational transformations often require more than successful change management. In contrast to change management, which is often about how to get from a well-defined point A to a well-defined point B, transformation usually requires the company to go from A to X. Instead of well-defined behavioral targets such as "use this tool" or "engage customers more directly," aspirations are often broader, such as "digital first" or "customer obsession." These then have to be translated appropriately for the local context of each department and team. This much tougher challenge requires speed, commitment, decentralization, and rapid learning curves. Extremely adaptive organizations achieve this by functioning more like an instant organization of networks than a hierarchy.

Think of start-ups in their scaling phase. The hierarchy and processes of a large company are fundamentally incompatible with high transformation speed. Instead, this requires informal, self-organizing networks that drive new strategic initiatives. These informal networks are governed by the collaborative advantage of a company. They bring the necessary creativity, decision-making speed, learning curve, and energization to the transformation (Fig. 7.2):

In most companies, this process is weak and erratic, as the political coalitions of transformation-oriented managers dominate any informal networks and are crippled by political conflicts. However, when managers become aware of the importance of collaborative advantage, they can activate it.

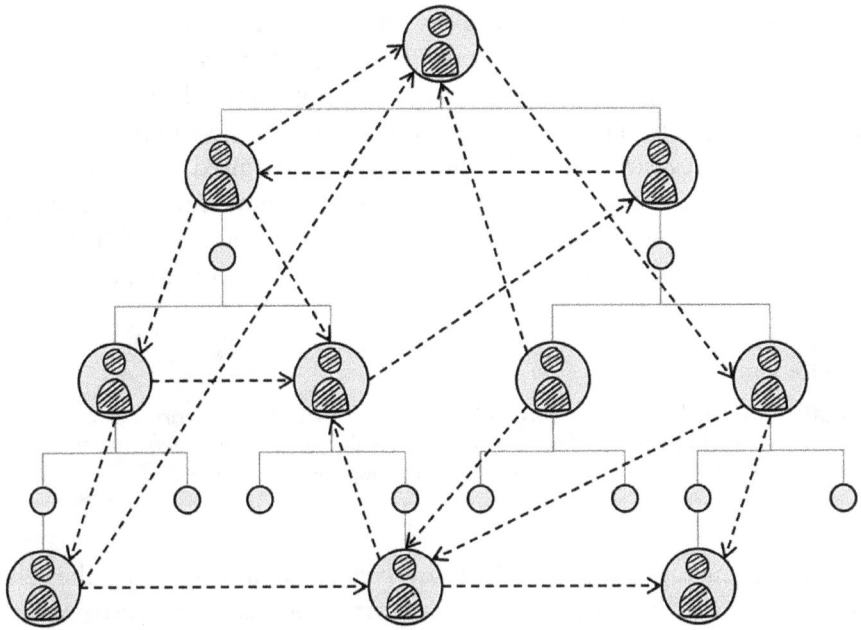

Fig. 7.2 Combination of formal hierarchy and flexible, boundary-spanning instant organization driven by personal relations

> *Leader's Voice: Jose Manuel Barroso on assembling a diverse coalition*
> *When we interviewed the former prime minister of Portugal and former president of the European Commission (EC), he impressed upon us the importance of bridging diverse viewpoints through empathy in order to achieve transformational change: "Succeeding in going through such demanding situations is a combination of hard work, trying to understand the tactical situation, and also invest time in the psychological aspects of the situation." In order to achieve this and become just the second president of the EC elected to a second term, Barroso highlighted the importance of perceiving subtle nuances of communication and speaking with each stakeholder in his own language: "Umberto Eco said one thing I never forgot. He said the language of Europe is translation, which is beautiful [...] It is not just about linguistics, it is about meaning."*

This insight is important for understanding the broader implications of the red balloon case. The twist is not that it is possible to get people to change their behavior and tackle a spontaneous task. It is that it is possible to get them to form effective, instant organizations, which coordinate themselves to achieve complicated tasks. Consider the example of the online encyclopedia Wikipedia, which was designed and implemented in much the same way as the red balloon challenge: By a volunteer army forming an instant organization based largely on the power of relational incentives.

To be clear, we're not suggesting replacing your normal hierarchies and structures altogether. These structures and hierarchies serve important functions in the legacy business, and although they might need to be adapted at some point in the transformation, they shouldn't be gotten rid of summarily. Instead, we propose complementing your formal hierarchy with a more flexible network that works in parallel to drive the transformation.

> **Quick Win:**
> Staff transformation teams should be based on expertise *and* on social influence. Transformation agents with broad credibility and easy personal access throughout the organization make transformations much faster.

Such instant organizations, which are created informally along the relational networks of key players of the transformation, have been instrumental in almost all the cases we have discussed so far. But let's look now at how such an instant organization can be created systematically in order to drive successful transformation.

At the dawn of the new millennium, IBM was convalescent after a near-death experience [10]. While Lou Gerstner had staved off disaster after catastrophic failures and the loss of over 150,000 jobs, incoming CEO Sam Palmisano inherited an organization with slowing growth, an increasingly irrelevant technology stack, and long product-to-market cycles, which hindered its commercialization efforts. New competitors often more successfully commercialized technology that IBM had pioneered, such as routers, web infrastructure, voice recognition, and RFID. These competitors, such as Cisco, Akami, and Nuance, were emerging from an agile start-up culture alien to IBM at the time. In addition, profitability was increasingly captured by companies providing wholesale solutions and taking on the complexity of integrating their technology into the business processes of their customers. In contrast, IBM's culture and employees were deeply rooted to the legacy of technology hardware. In short, IBM was in desperate need of a transformation to stay relevant.

IBM achieved this between 2000 and 2008. Instead of providing legacy products rooted in hardware and software, it moved much closer to the customer and provided business value in consulting, analytics, and industry-specific solutions. This allowed IBM to get ahead of a wave of disruptions that badly hit many of its one-time competitors, such as HP, Dell, and Sun.

By 2010, revenues had increased to about $100 billion and profitability had gone up substantially.

The success of this transformation was powered by flexible instant organization based on a network of transformation agents. Specifically, Palmisano brought overlapping teams of strategic leaders together in so-called Strategic Leadership Forums (SLFs). These were inspired by GE's Work-Outs but focused on kickstarting transformative initiatives and re-shaping strategic decision-making, making the initiatives exploratory rather than part of an incremental legacy business.

The SLFs were three and a half days each and facilitated by senior business school faculty. They created a cohesive and energized team of teams, with each group formulating its own transformation gap statement and working largely autonomously, and with discipline, on achieving these initiatives. The SLFs also identified cultural challenges for the transformations and proposed interventions for the full community. During the SLFs, cross-functional groups from different departments came together and engaged in disciplined problem-solving as modeled and coached by the business school professors.

> **Lesson Learned:**
> A successful transformation requires effective, cross-functional instant organizations that are self-coordinated and focused on achieving self-formulated transformation challenges in collaborative sprints.

Transformation initiatives focused on revamping the internal culture of IBM included a renewal of the strategy process toward a strategy-as-dialogue approach, and the breakdown of structural barriers between departments that needed to collaborate more closely in order to develop integrated solutions instead of isolated products. The senior leadership team was expanded to three teams with overlapping memberships, so that a central interface for coordination could be formed. You might be reminded of the networked structure of the economic development board behind Singapore's economic transformation. Through the initiatives of this network, IBM managed to achieve a successful transformation for the second time in its history.

IBM's experience illustrates the importance of nurturing a flexible instant organization by carefully creating and empowering the right networks. In other words, it illustrates an application of collaborative advantage in order to kickstart and steer a transformation initiative. But can this approach be scaled from a flexible network that spans strategic decision-makers to encompass an entire global organization? It has been—and in the most unlikely of places: A manufacturer steeped in detail-obsessed, technocratic German engineering culture.

7.9 Combine Internal and External Collaborative Structures

Daimler looks back on a long and proud history of product excellence and technological superiority. However, the carmaker's traditional business model, centered around selling internal combustion engine (ICE)-powered cars, is increasingly under threat. Growing global awareness of climate risks, mounting regulatory as well as social pressure, and technological advances are pushing the market away from ICEs and toward electric vehicles (EVs). In addition, advances in autonomous driving and emerging trends of ride-hailing and car-sharing services signal a shift away from the car as a technologically differentiated product you own and toward mobility as a service. Taken together, these trends are pushing Daimler to compete in unfamiliar markets, eroding the competitive relevance of its carefully groomed core capabilities.

The company, however, chose not to bury heads in the sand; it took the challenge head-on: "Our goal for Daimler and the entire team is not just to somehow survive the upheaval in the automotive industry—but to shape it," said Dieter Zetsche, CEO of Daimler between 2006 and 2019. "We are driving change today so that we will not be driven tomorrow.", as.

In recent years, Lab1886 has been a cornerstone of this transformation. Named for the year the automobile was invented (Carl Benz applied for a patent for his "vehicle powered by a gas engine" on January 29, 1886), Lab1886's goal is to facilitate cross-divisional and cross-company collaboration to enable the company to compete in these new areas. Through this platform, Daimler "intrapreneurs" have developed solutions such as the mobility app moovel and "Mercedes me," digital access to the Mercedes-Benz world, 2nd Use-Batterystorage, and Van2share. However, the initiative that most clearly illustrates Lab1886's approach and impact is car2go.

One of the lab's first business innovation projects, car2go revolutionized the car-sharing market from its inception. The Daimler subsidiary became the international market leader in flexible car sharing. Around 2.7 million customers have used the approximately 14,000 smart and Mercedes-Benz vehicles more than 84 million times. Every 1.4 seconds, a car2go vehicle is rented somewhere in the world. While car2Go and Share Now were later sold to Stellantis, they remain among the few large, pioneering digital business models successfully launched by European manufacturers. Daimler board member Bodo Uebber summarized the importance of Lab1886 as follows: "For ten years, Business Innovation has been driving new ideas and projects that continue the pioneering spirit of our founders and promote the culture of innovation throughout the group. With Lab1886, we are continuing this success story. We intelligently combine our business with agile methods and unconventional approaches from the start-up world to successfully develop new and innovative business models to market maturity."

How does Lab1886 do what it does? The platform works in three stages: For the first stage, ideation, every employee has the chance to hand in their ideas. Through crowd voting, a funding round, and a "shark tank," ideas with the greatest potential are identified. In the next phase, incubation, the projects selected by the shark tank are piloted and developed to market maturity. The employees who generated the ideas are supported in developing them through professional mentoring, supervision by specialists for complex challenges, co-working spaces and workshops, financial support, and an inspiring working atmosphere. During development, the employees are also released from their other duties to be able to fully concentrate on their project within a "swarm" team. Following a successful incubation phase, the newly developed products or new services face the challenges of the global market in the third phase, commercialization. Here, initiatives are rolled out with the goal of either re-integrating them later as semi-autonomous business units of Daimler or spinning them off. Either way, the employee-founders of these initiatives have substantial equity in the venture.

> **Self-Reflection:**
> Think about building your own "Lab1886" to facilitate cross-company collaboration: What would it take you to set up a platform based on these three stages of ideation, incubation, and commercialization? Try to write an action plan, defining the steps you could take to create such an initiative.

While Daimler's approach was well executed, it may not appear to be radically different from how many other intrapreneurship programs work. So why has Lab1886 consistently created transformative new lines of business while so many intrapreneurship programs struggle to make an impact? We would suggest the answer lies in Lab1886's collaboration signature. Specifically, it has both a flexible *internal* instant organization capability and open networks to crucial *external* resources.

Start with the internal resources. Crucial to the internal collaboration signature of Daimler are the aforementioned "swarm organizations." These are temporary project teams made up of employees from different departments who can freely choose a form and hierarchy for solving specific problems. With this initiative, thinking in silos is reduced and employees get to contribute to solving various challenges across the company—which also leads to higher identification with the group. Daimler aims to have a quarter of its employees working in these swarm organizations. This initiative was kickstarted with a game-changer swarm team, in which twenty high-value members advised and supported the business units, together with agile coaches, to introduce the swarm concept. The Leadership2020 team was also crucial to shaping the internal collaboration signature: 144 ambassadors with diverse backgrounds and management levels were brought into the company to increase agility and speed across the people, processes, and culture of Daimler. Eight main topics were defined and one topic leader each was selected among the ambassadors, as well as an executive sponsor.

But the aim was to create bottom-up innovation and change initiative—with the help of the ambassadors or agility coaches if needed. These broader programs are supported and anchored with simple, tangible practices—such as Lunch&Learn. In 30-minute keynote speeches, employees present their colleagues with current projects, show and test new methods and tools, or exchange ideas on topics that give people a look beyond their own cubicle.

Consider how the internal collaboration signature nurtured by these initiatives synergizes with the approach of the Lab1886: Instead of colliding with rigid hierarchies in the business units, Lab1886 projects can build on the vast resources and knowledge intrinsic to the Daimler organization. This is in part because the business units have existing networks built around flexible, boundary-spanning collaborations. These flexible networks span all the way through the corporate hierarchy: "Promising employee projects have been given permanent access to us managers. We then have regular meetings or even short phone calls in between or brief shout-outs as needed. This allowed us to bring together the resources and contacts that were important for the team to take the next steps," Martin Zimmermann, CSO at Daimler, told us. In practice, this means that senior board members regularly personally sponsor and advise swarm projects started by employees five or six reporting levels below them. Through these different nudges toward internal collaboration, Daimler has built the foundation that positions the Lab1886 teams to succeed: Rather than being foreign bodies in a hierarchical organization, the swarm teams and the Lab1886 teams can unleash potential.

> **Quick Win:**
>
> Prepare your organization for successful *internal* collaboration
>
> - Facilitate and incentivize the work in temporary project teams with employees from different departments ("swarm organizations"), where employees can solve problems of their interest in line with the overall transformation vision
> - Think about bringing "ambassadors" into your organization with diverse backgrounds and management levels to increase agility and speed and to support these swarm organizations
> - Foster the exchange about the projects your employees are currently working on in their teams through initiatives that allow them to briefly present their projects and get feedback from their peers
> - Sponsor promising employee projects from the top to reward and motivate employees for their work and ideas

Of course, external interfaces also play a crucial role at Daimler. Take, as an example, their Start-up Autobahn platform. Daimler launched this initiative to infuse decades of expertise with a start-up and founder spirit—and gift start-ups and founders with rich experience. Through this platform, start-ups are connected not only with Daimler itself but also with other corporate partners. After a thorough screening, the thirty most "future-driven" start-ups are selected and are able to work jointly on concepts and prototypes with established corporate units. Every team gets a mentor, and at the end, all projects are presented at an expo day, where the start-ups come together with Daimler, other corporate partners, investors, researchers, and developers. The goal during each phase is to promote integration of or investment in future-driven projects. As Susannah Hahn, Managing Director of 1886Venture, explained: "We work with a wide variety of areas and departments in the group and across all functions: development, production, sales et cetera. One example: We launched the Start-up Autobahn project together with external partners and with R&D. This is an initiative that had the goal of bringing the world's best mobility start-ups to the Stuttgart location—that is, to act like a magnet. Within the last two years, Europe's largest mobility start-up platform has emerged from this, with over twenty partners in the meantime. The goal was to attract investors, create a mentor network and offer the start-ups the opportunity to pitch to an interesting audience."

This spirit of opening up interfaces also extends beyond the boundaries of Lab1886. "Stop talking – Start hacking" was the slogan of the 24-hour @HACK.IAA that Mercedes-Benz developers staged at the world's largest motor show in Frankfurt." We are one of the first automotive manufacturers to give external software developers around the world access to our own Mercedes-Benz Mobile Software Development Kit," said Sajjad Khan, executive vice president "The SDK provides access to various programming interfaces to the vehicle. Of course, the focus is once again on security, one of the central core values of Mercedes-Benz." The aim was to make greater use of the creative potential of external developers in the future. Thus, external experts and inspirations were incorporated into the company to generate radically new ideas.

> **Quick Win:**
>
> Prepare your organization for successful *external* collaboration
>
> - Open your doors to start-ups in your area of business by offering them collaborations that are beneficial for both sides: they bring the agile founder spirit and you offer them expertise and execution power
> - Set up initiatives (e.g. Hackathons, other competitions) that allow you to include ideas from external experts (e.g. software developers) into your organization. Not everything needs to be solved internally

In sum, Daimler created a flexible network in order to drive their successful transformation. Their collaboration signature was transformed internally through the use of swarm organizations and the Leadership2020 initiative, but also opened up externally, for example through the Start-Up Autobahn. Lab1886 served as a focal point to gather and synergize potential into tangible renewal and create substantial new business along the way.

Crucially, the collaborative advantage behind Daimler's transformation was enabled by value-added collaborations that spanned internal silos as well as organizational boundaries. The transformation was powered by a dynamic network spanning internal and external boundaries. In other words: an instant organization powered by collaborative advantage.

An interesting idea for how to kickstart these networks is the innovation campaign. As we learned from the chief technology officer of Bühler, a manufacturing company, innovation campaigns often produce only low-quality outputs in the first iterations, especially if not supported by a larger initiative. What they do provide, however, is an address list of employees who care about innovation at the organization and put in their own time toward shaping the company's future. The address list is a great resource to kickstart your volunteer army and form a network of instant organizations to shape your transformation.

> *Leaders' voice: Alexander Birken and the secret sauce behind the only mail-order company to thrive through digitalization*
>
> *"I refuse to measure what this culture transformation costs." When Alexander Birken told us about this guidance from him at the start of the transformation journey at Otto Group, a globally operating e-commerce and service group with a history as a venerable German mail-order retailer, we were honestly perplexed. Afterall, as e-commerce companies often operate on razor-thin margins, in our experience everything seems to be driven by cost-consciousness in this industry. But then again, pretty much every other mail-order retailer went bankrupt during the ascent of the internet and Otto Group thrived, so maybe the jovial north German was onto something.*
>
> *In approaching his transformation, Birken was very conscious in choosing an iterative and continuous approach rather than an immediate radical departure to transformation: He didn't want massive employee turnover but for everybody to be part of the change. Through his collaborative approach, he was soon able to nurture a coalition throughout the organization completely committed to making Otto Group fit for the digital future: "We were very fortunate to early achieve complete alignment between the executive board and our majority shareholders for this journey. On an operational level, we got our corporate influencers and key players on board through a variety of workshops."*
>
> *Birken highlighted a few key themes which made the transformation at Otto successful: A collaborative approach which distributed ownership widely, a primacy of speed over perfection, total focus on the needs of real customers over abstract strategy, and synergies in leveraging the entire Otto group for each initiative.*
>
> *The transformation process was kickstarted simultaneously top-down and bottom-up at Otto. On the top management side, the transformation was initiated with the shareholders and executive board together on stage (live-streamed to the entire company), thinking together how to reinvent the culture. Simultaneously, he initiated a variety of bottom-up workstreams throughout the company which were tasked with developing their own vision of how Otto Group was to work in the future. These workstreams were free to organize themselves—and even set their own goals. "That there was no pre-defined program goal led to big shocks all around," Birken told us laughingly. For each workstream, members of the board functioned as "god-fathers": These were responsible for removing barriers and finding budgets as well as functioning as sparring partners, but were not the "boss" of the workstream.*

"It was a great change also for us in the board, how we collaborate together and the culture we live and role-model for the rest of the organization," Birken told us. He likens the process to couples therapy rather than a workshop: *"We worked with a psychologist not for a few workshops, but once every month for years on end."* Through this *"therapeutic"* process, they were able to transform the way they collaborated: *"A key experience happened in one of the board meetings in Hamburg where we were discussing strategy in a break. A huge escalation between the alpha animals. After almost two hours of reflection of this incident with the psychologist, I was deeply ashamed of myself. But only by going through the pain and really questioning ourselves could we really develop the culture we needed."*

Progress was slow at first: *"At the first fuck up night we organized, half of the managers shared real fuck-ups, the other half was more curated impression management. But it became better every time."* Overall, the transformation at Otto Group was driven in a very decentral way: While there was a central roster of topic coaches, ownership for the workstreams was distributed locally, and the workstreams were staffed cross-functional, with members spanning workers council, business units, and board members. Birken likened the culture change project management to modern programming: *"There was no hierarchy, but also no anarchy. We are driven by alignment around results, not authority."* The main issue here was the development of trust: *"The times are over when the CEO had the answers. I don't know the answers – the answers are deep in my organization. I have to create a culture where the right answers are unearthed from within."* For Birken, this meant he had to learn to celebrate the loss of control. For example, he was vehemently opposed to the idea of evaluating the progress of the transformation with culture surveys. His culture team however basically told him at a board meeting *"we don't care you don't want to do a survey, we believe in the value and will do it anyways."* When presented with the results of the survey, he had to admit that it produced a lot of value.

Through this unusual approach, Birken managed one of the most remarkable transformations of an incumbent in the face of digitalization we have witnessed. While corporate revenues rose substantially, the most important success indicators for Birken are more qualitative. These can be large, for example, the fact that the incumbent Otto Group was able to build and grow the internal start-up About You to unicorn status. But they can also be in the operational details: For example, when the Corona pandemic made the fulfillment of orders to end-customers potentially hazardous, a frontline employee came up with a solution to certify the delivery of orders without any need for physical contact. Just a few days later, the solution was operable throughout the Otto group and its partners. In Birken's view, this would have never been possible without the transformation.

Quick Win:
Frame the clear need for the transformation and then distribute ownership to motivated employees very early on: How can we live the new vision? As employees reach out to stakeholders and generate ideas, they naturally buy into the transformation and develop pride of ownership.

References

In order to keep the book lean enough to comfortably be read on a plane, we have listed the full references on the companion website for your convenience. If you want to dig deeper, please check them out here:

1. Collaborative-advantage.org/references-transformation/1.
2. Collaborative-advantage.org/references-transformation/2.
3. Collaborative-advantage.org/references-transformation/3.
4. Collaborative-advantage.org/references-transformation/4.
5. Collaborative-advantage.org/references-transformation/5.
6. Collaborative-advantage.org/references-transformation/6.
7. Collaborative-advantage.org/references-transformation/7.
8. Collaborative-advantage.org/references-transformation/8.
9. Collaborative-advantage.org/references-transformation/9.
10. Collaborative-advantage.org/references-transformation/10.

8

Leveraging Partnerships for Transformation

> *Leadership is the capacity to translate vision into reality.*
> —Warren Bennis

8.1 Apply Collaborative Practices to Maintain Your Advantage as You Grow

When we discuss collaborative advantage management and relational transformations with leaders, many of them come from one of two positions. First, there are leaders from new ventures who are wondering how to keep the secret sauce flowing in the face of breakneck growth. How to stay bold and innovative rather than become complacent in the face of their own success? The second group has the opposite problem in some ways: How to rejuvenate a struggling incumbent?

Given these two very different starting points, you would think our prescriptions would be very different. But they are not.

Ed Catmull is the president and co-founder of the movie studio Pixar. Well into his seventies, the soft-spoken, thoughtful man with an impressive beard could hardly be more different from his luminary counterpart, Steve Jobs. Pixar started out with a bang with *Toy Story*, a resounding success that flushed the young company's coffers with $360 million. But as many of the leaders of successful new ventures can attest, this is really only where the problems start. Catmull: "So the question was, okay, how do you make it so that it's sustainable? Because the people I knew who were in these [failed] companies—and I had a lot of friends in Silicon Valley—were smart, and they were creative, and they were hardworking. So, whatever the problem was actually leading them astray was really hard to see, and the implication was, whatever that force was, it would also apply to us at Pixar. So, this became the interesting question. These forces are at work; can we find them before they do us in? So, at the end of the year, I realized that this is actually the next goal. It's not a film. It's how we can have an environment where we can find and address these problems."

As you might expect, we have our own ideas about what this mysterious force of Catmull's might be. And whether he would label it as we do, his response worked: Over the coming decade, Pixar would produce 17 feature films that raked in on average more than half a billion dollars at the box office each and collectively earned 13 academy awards.

How did Catmull achieve this? [11]

We would argue it has something to do with his clear focus on and particular approach to managing the collaborative advantage of his organization. To illustrate his focus on the collaborative advantage at Pixar, take the company's Brooklyn headquarters—by many accounts one of the most beautiful office buildings ever designed, let alone built: A sunlit box of glass and wood equipped with speakeasy, fireplaces, a roof deck, and café. You would expect Catmull to be beaming with pride about this crown jewel. You would be wrong. Catmull: "In fact, this building was a mistake. The reason it was a mistake is that it doesn't create the kind of interactions we need to create. We should have made the hallways wider. We should have made the café bigger, to draw more people. We should have put the offices around the edges to create more shared space in the center."

Given these priorities, we can understand approach to Pixar's challenges more broadly. In successful groups, one of the biggest relational challenges is keeping groups flexible enough to question themselves, admit mistakes, and correct their course. It's about being able to admit being wrong. And in such an innovation-centric and uncertain environment as the movie industry, this is even more the case than usual. Again, Catmull: "All the movies are bad at first. (…). I'm not saying that in a modest way. I was in the meetings. I saw the early versions, and they were bad. Really bad. (…) The goal is to get the team right, get them moving in the right direction, and get them to see where they are making mistakes and where they are succeeding."

Unsurprisingly, Catmull spends an inordinate amount of time monitoring the collaboration signature at Pixar: "Mostly you can feel it in the room.

When a team isn't working, you see defensive body language, or you see people close down. Or there's just silence. The ideas stop coming, or they can't see the problem. [...] But it becomes harder and harder as time goes on, because as directors get more experienced, they sometimes have a harder time hearing other points of view that might help them. [...] So, you have to create mechanisms where teams of people can keep working together to see what's really happening, and then work together to solve problems."

> **Self-Reflection:**
> Observe the teams in your organization: How are they working together? What's the body language of your employees? Is there silence or interaction in the room?

Catmull has established a couple of key practices to keep the collaboration flowing freely through the organization. In "dailies," all employees gather, regardless of department or rank, to view the previous day's footage and provide feedback and impressions. Project teams go on field trips to immerse themselves as a group in the environment of the film—scuba diving for *Finding Nemo*, archery lessons for the *Brave* team. "BrainTrust" meetings are a core feature of Pixar's culture. Here, teams of the company's top storyteller provide regular, vigorously candid outside-in feedback on films in development. Pixar University, meanwhile, offers a diverse array of courses, from fencing to painting to tai chi. This allows people from different areas of the company to mix—and form personal connections that span structural fault lines. Finally, in "postmortems," Catmull takes film teams to offsite retreats after completion of a film to share and capture their biggest learnings from the process. Collectively, these practices serve to create a deep web of relationships that disrupt groupthink and establish norms and trusted veins for unbiased feedback and sometimes-radical course corrections.

Catmull's relational priorities have also informed his personal leadership approach. For example, he is deeply involved in onboarding new employees and connecting them with others throughout the organization. He joins BrainTrust meetings and scans the interactions for signs of relational troubles or progress. He prioritizes developing back-channel communication throughout the organization to find out what is happening behind the scenes. His worries tend to center more around awkward silences and people avoiding each other than missed deadlines. On the flipside, he openly celebrates when groups jointly take initiative without asking permission.

> **Quick Win:**
>
> How to keep collaboration flowing through your organization:
>
> - Daily gatherings of employees to informally reflect on the previous day's work including feedback and goals for the upcoming day
> - Field trips for project teams to enhance their sense of connection
> - Regular cross-company feedback sessions on current projects and ideas
> - Educational offerings for employees to learn new skills and practice them together (e.g. sports, arts, science)
> - Reflection offsites after the completion of a project to reflect on the biggest learnings
> - Onboarding processes that directly connect new employees throughout the organization
> - Leadership involvement in the above-mentioned suggestions to remove the barriers between leaders and employees and celebrate initiative

The continued success of Pixar might illustrate the potential of a relational management approach to tackling that first challenge—growing without losing the can-do, start-up feel of a place—but what about the second? It might not seem radical enough to rejuvenate a declining incumbent. Lucky for us, Catmull's tale would come to address this, too.

8.2 Bring Collaborative Practices to New Organizations

> In matters of style, swim with the current; in matters of principle, stand like a rock.—Thomas Jefferson

Disney Animations was struggling. After the roaring successes of the nineteen-nineties, a series of dull (and unprofitable) movies had damaged the studio's reputation. By 2006, Disney CEO Bob Iger decided something had to be done. Disney bought Pixar, and he put Catmull in charge of revitalizing Disney Animations.

Observers didn't have high hopes. First, there was the huge size difference between Pixar and Disney. An article in Fortune at the time likened the challenge to "Nemo swallowing the whale." Second, there was the geographical distance between the studios' headquarters, each on one U.S. coast, which would seem to stymie cultural cross-fertilization.

Catmull characteristically uttered about two sentences at an all-hands event with the anxious Disney employees: "We're not going to turn Disney into a clone of Pixar. What we are going to do is build a studio on your talent and passion." So far, so uncontroversial. But how could Catmull apply his relational principles and experiences to Disney Animations?

Start with physical structure. At the time of the acquisition, Disney employees were scattered across four floors of a giant building. This siloed them in groups based on technical expertise (animations, layout, designs) rather than their collaborative function. This didn't fit Catmull's vision; he ordered a rebuild that gathered all creative and technical employees together in a central "town center" called the caffeine patch. Instead of isolating himself on an executive floor, he put his own office right there in the center, to ensure maximum availability and connectivity.

> **Self-Reflection:**
> Think about your organization's physical spaces. Does your office structure foster or hinder cross-functional and cross-company collaboration?

Catmull also redefined roles and processes. Before the Disney-Pixar deal, the movie creation process at Disney Animations was executive-centric: executives created development teams who designed stories. Executives also evaluated these ideas, decided which ones should be pursued, and assigned teams to those. Catmull put this entire philosophy on its head, changing to a director-centric approach instead. In this model, directors are the ones coming up with their own ideas. They develop these and pitch them. In this model, executives are far less powerful and fulfill a more servile leadership role, supporting directors instead of reigning above them. Field trips to Pixar BrainTrusts let Disney employees see people just like them making this approach work in the real world.

> **Quick Win:**
> Try the following experiment: Tell your project leaders to ask their team members to come up with ideas for the next project—ideas they should pitch in an upcoming team meeting. A proven framework is the 5 × 5 × 5 project: projects that can be tested within five days of work, that cost no more than $5000, but which have the potential to generate (or save) at least $500,000 USD in their first year. Then, as a team, decide on one such experiment to pursue.

The changes in Disney's collaboration signatures were quickly noted by its employees: "A breath of fresh air" and "like the fall of the Berlin Wall!" Talk about relational barriers coming down! These feelings were made tangible in financial performance. By the 2010s, Disney was achieving Pixar-level success: Tangled (a $591 million box office), Wreck-It Ralph ($471 million), Frozen ($1.2 billion), Big Hero 6 ($657 million), and Zootopia ($931 million)—to name just a few.

In our view, however, among the most amazing pieces of this transformation was that there was almost zero turnover amid all of this change. For a final word, Catmull (though with our emphasis): "The people who made these films are the same people who were there when they were failing. We put in some new systems, *they learned new ways of interacting*, and they changed their behavior, and now they are a completely different group of people when they work together." We couldn't have asked for a nicer synopsis of collaborative advantage.

So far, we have mostly pointed out how organizations have managed their collaboration signatures in order to drive organic transformations. But for many companies, acquisitions provide an interesting short-cut to transformation. They bring in new capabilities and establish market positions much more quickly than in-house efforts could. From a relational perspective, they are also a powerful tool for changing the relational structure of an organization and bringing in powerful coalitions that embody a new mindset. However, M&A's mixed track record points to the difficulty of managing this process well.

8.3 Combine Autonomy and Synergy to Leverage the Transformation Potential of Acquisitions

To understand how acquisitions may inspire transformations and the relevant relational principles, let's look at Springer. One of Germany's traditional publishing houses, Axel Springer and its business model were fundamentally disrupted by the advent of the internet. Journalism moved online and the circulation halved. Correspondingly, advertisement revenues fell off a cliff, and many publishers reacted with mass layoffs. In the U.S., the number of journalism jobs fell from around 56,000 in 2000 to only 36,700 in 2013.

Leader's Voice: Mathias Döpfner Axel Springer CEO Mathias Döpfner might seem an unlikely candidate to have led the company through a successful transformation in a time of upheaval. In fact, many doubted him, not least because he was just 39 when he took the helm; he'd also studied music and theater rather than finance or marketing. Döpfner describes the resistance he met when embarking on his transformation journey: "The young man has to make his experiences," his managers said skeptically, treating his initiative like a student research project. Yet Döpfner proved his critiques wrong with one of the most successful digital transformations in the journalism and publishing industry. By 2015, Springer's new digital offerings accounted for more than 60 percent of revenues and boasted higher profitability than other divisions, accounting for nearly 70 percent of earnings. The company posted record EBITDA in every post-transformation year but one.

After laying out his vision for Axel Springer to become "the winner of digitalization in European media business," Döpfner proceeded to transform the company at breakneck speed through acquisitions. He knew that the rules for the digital world were completely different than those of traditional print publishing. He told us how he made use of his expertise and background in order to overcome the resistance he faced: "As a former editor-in chief myself, I knew the ins and outs of the business. So, when people mounted excuses, I knew when I could tell them: Guys, I know this is in fact possible." He credits his ability to energize the transformation with his personality: "I was the doomsday prophet-in-chief. I am a pessimist on purpose, I really could paint a picture of all the ways the company could fail. The very focused way in which I sent out this message, together with the first successes, really helped kickstart the movement, which made the transformation successful."

By acquiring young, innovative, digital start-ups, Döpfner could push his company toward the necessary capabilities, mindsets, and assets for competing in a transformed competitive landscape. He did so with incredible energy: Between 2006 and 2013, he averaged one acquisition every four weeks. These purchases ranged from segment-agnostic buys to segment-specific deals. (The former are acquisitions that primarily focus on media-related business models, but are not necessarily related to one of the traditional revenue streams of the publishing world. Segment-specific acquisitions focus on the revenue pillars of the traditional publishing world, such as classified ad portals.) Of course, not everybody was happy with the pace of change: "Where people were obstructing the transformation, I had to draw the consequences. Managers who integrated the digital business were rewarded, managers who blocked them were let go. This meant, for example, that five of the six members of the executive board I started with had to go."

He centered his transformation strategy around three core principles: First, no fear of cannibalization of the print business by online offerings. Second, *acceptance of different entrepreneurial personalities. Third, prohibition of silo thinking. These provide a window into his thinking about the relational interplay between new digital acquisitions and legacy print. He explained to us his unusual approach to integrating his new acquisitions:* "I believe that formal reporting lines and standardized processes would kill the entrepreneurial energy of our start-ups. Instead, we really doubled down on a decentral approach to be able to maintain the digital talent we needed." *The success of this approach can be seen in his acquisition of Idealo, which grew within Springer from seven employees to 1200, and is still growing (profitably) 60 percent a year.*

Döpfner provided the newcomers ample freedom and safe spaces to grow their business and reinforce their digital-first culture. At the same time, the goal was not to have them completely separated from the core organization. Döpfner explained: "To ensure that all of the company's more than 14,000 employees potentially have a chance to participate and contribute ideas, we said very early on that we would not build the digital business as a separate silo, but as an integral part. This means that every employee in this company is responsible for digitization." *Silos were to be avoided, and the relational impact of the digital entrepreneurs should transform the legacy operation. He gave Springer's tabloid Bild and its digital twin, Bild.de, as an example:* "In the beginning we separated the two: 80 percent of the meetings with the managers were the print executives explaining to me that their circulation was falling because Bild.de was taking their readers away. So, I changed it and had one lead responsible for both stabilizing print and growing digital. Now the meetings were all about how he was growing the digital offering based on print content and building synergies between the two. As soon as we had a critical mass here, everybody become proud mothers and fathers of the digital success stories."

Did all of this theory work in practice? Through Springer's holding structure, operational independence was secured for the new acquisitions. Döpfner also made a point of retaining the founders and senior managers after the acquisition. He told us that, to achieve this, he had to radically transform the incentive system at Springer: "We had to align incentives in order to keep the best entrepreneurs. That often meant that successful internal entrepreneurs would substantially out-earn members the members of the executive board they reported to." *Together, these approaches allowed the acquired companies to maintain their distinctive cultural identity and internal collaboration signature, which in turn maintained growth momentum without being held back by the unwieldy legacy business. This approach of trusting founders to develop their companies further while providing resources in true partnership was key to Döpfner's approach:* "Maximum tolerance for other corporate cultures. We offer the synergies that our company has in the family network as a toolbox. Every company at Axel Springer can use these tools to run its business, to place advertising, to exploit economies of scale via cross-promotion. There is the sales *organization, which helps us to sell products better, and the international infrastructure, which helps us to internationalize. There is know-how, especially IT know-how, and financial resources. Anyone in the Axel Springer family who has a need may help themselves. Anyone who thinks they can run their business better without all this can also do everything on their own. We'll leave him alone as long as he stays within the budget."*

But if these acquisitions were so independent, how could they help transform Springer's legacy business? Similar to the case at Daimler, this required building a foundation. Only if the organization has a capacity to absorb new ideas and practices will it be possible for acquisitions to push it forward. Döpfner developed a strategy focused on creativity, entrepreneurship, and integrity. To ensure that the new strategy was implemented across the legacy business, the company had more than fifty workshops and every manager took part in at least one. In addition, managers were given the opportunity (via an anonymous survey) to question their own leadership behavior, learn more about their own strengths and weaknesses, and work with coaches individually on improvements. Concrete practices were also implemented in order to anchor these ideas across the organization. For example, Springer sends key employees for three-six months to Silicon Valley as part of a program called "visiting fellows." In a format called pizza connection, employees can learn more about new topics and also share their own knowledge over lunch.

Döpfner recognized the challenge of this parallel approach: "The Group structure consisted of around 90 percent losers (i.e. print) and around 10 percent winners (i.e. digital). By virtue of their superior numbers alone, the losers were in a position to refuse and fight down the transformation. So a shared responsibility between the two areas had to be created in order to gain support from the print side." In order to help everyone understand the growing importance of the digital business to group revenues, the digital result was included in the target agreements of many employees at an early stage. This motivated the broad mass of Axel Springer employees to commit to the digital transformation process. The basic idea here was always: No winners or losers from digitization; instead, everyone participates in the successes of the new business. Furthermore, Döpfner was convinced that progressive digitization would succeed best if executives assumed cross-media responsibility. BILD'S then editor-in-chief, Kai Diekmann, also became publisher of Bild.de. Relational incentives and connections were forged that allowed the digital acquisitions to project their influence into the legacy business. Döpfner: "We are creating an integrated hierarchy pyramid, at the end of which there is a boss who is responsible for both digital and analogue, whether it's content, technology, ads and advertising marketing. At the core, I think, was the key factor that changed our corporate culture toward digitization. Suddenly, there were all winners. Everyone here in the company is responsible for digitizing their business model, their brand, their

> content. And therefore everyone was also responsible for the successful digital transformation. And that is how we are driving digital transformation forward together today. [...] There are many seemingly small things [that we can learn from the start-up world] and very important ones: speed in decision-making and implementation, direct responsibility, flat hierarchies and uncomplicated forms of communication, greater technological know-how, an open and modern corporate culture."
>
> A prime example of such an interface is the Axel Springer Plug and Play Incubator. In 2013, Springer joined forces with the US company "Plug and Play Tech Center" to establish an accelerator to promote start-ups in Berlin. From this point on, Springer also invested in early-stage start-ups, providing the group with valuable insights into innovative technologies, contact with promising talents, and stakes in promising companies. It connected start-up founders and group executives, giving them a chance to learn from each other. Since 2013, more than 100 companies have been supported by Springer. "It is important for Axel Springer to be 'infected' by the way start-ups make decisions. These young companies make far-reaching and binding decisions every week, which—if they are wrong—have lasting effects on the future success of the company," says Döpfner. "In a corporation like ours, employees rarely have the opportunity to actually experience the importance of accountability and liability in all its consequences. But this is helpful if they want to realize the extent of their own freedoms." Such early-stage investments can pay off in several ways—whether through integration of the start-up into the existing corporate structure, or by selling shares in a successful group, or even in the case of failures, by avoiding the mistakes Springer could witness at close hand.
>
> The relational approach to using acquisitions to transform a legacy business—without quashing the acquired company's autonomy—can take many forms, sometimes even architectural. Döpfner: "We want to build a new house here in Berlin, right next to our existing building. A Media Campus that will set new standards for collaboration and communication not only through its architecture, but also through the new definition of office space in a dematerialized digital world. This building will primarily house the new digital offerings and network even more closely with the classic brands from our company."
>
> Döfner's approach made Axel Springer one of the few success stories in the digital transformation of legacy print organizations. It changed the company from a regional player in a declining and disrupted industry to a global media powerhouse with the sixth widest reach worldwide.

Analyzing and managing your collaboration signatures can aid post-merger integration. We see more and more innovative approaches being developed to understand how internal fault lines develop out of pre-merger boundaries—and how they can be overcome. This includes using natural language processing algorithms to identify the degree to which employees stick to old operating logics versus developing a new, shared identity. We will return to a more detailed discussion of this later, when we provide some practical pointers for how to use relational analytics to steer and support transformations.

8.4 Three Take-Aways for Managers

From individual incentives to peer persuasion. Behavior changes and new ways of making decisions are dependent on local social dynamics: Employees orient themselves on trusted peers rather than rousing leadership talks.

> **Quick Win:**
> Relational incentives are a powerful tool for designing peer engagement around your change agenda (think back to the Red Balloon Challenge). This way, the social fabric supports rather than hinders change.

Social activism. The most successful transformation initiatives are not driven by formal project management and stage-gate processes. Rather, a flexible and self-organizing network creatively drives and coordinates local initiatives, as we have seen in the cases of Covestro, Daimler, and IBM.

> **Quick Win:**
> Relational management of transformations is much more like starting a social movement than managing a construction project. Focus on social dynamics to kickstart change and implement data-driven feedback-loops to self-correct during development, rather than invest too much time in detailed planning.

Mergers and Transformation. We have repeatedly seen organizations use acquisitions not only to build new market positions and acquire capabilities, but also to kickstart transformation by providing direct exposure to new ways of working.

> **Quick Win:**
>
> Think beyond organic transformation. Each acquisition is a moment to shake up the relational nervous system of your organization, and thus its decision-making architecture. This requires careful management of the post-merger integration process.

8.5 Ideas for Action: Simple Practices

Relational Learning. Align your management through immersive learning trips. Consider how VM required supervisory board members to join expeditions to Japan to learn about lean production principles. Similarly, consider how Springer had senior journalists work in Silicon Valley to immerse themselves in digital start-up culture.

Brain Trust. Take a page out of Pixar's playbook and establish a network of senior experts who provide focused and concise feedback on development projects throughout the organization. These meetings tend to be most candid and, accordingly, effective when the management of the project in question is absent and clear peer feedback can be provided without political concerns.

Influencer Marketing. Identify local informal influencers and incorporate them as change champions in your transformation drive. Often, these are not formal leaders but experienced and trusted experts whom their colleagues turn to whenever a problem is particularly tricky. By connecting and empowering these influencers, as Covestro did, the resources you invest in driving your transformation initiative will have outsized returns.

Relational Incentives. Capitalize on the power of peer relationships by employing peer-based incentives. Consider rewarding employees based on innovative behaviors not from themselves but from close peers. A more limited approach was Springer's early decision to make the performance of the new digital unit part of everybody's variable compensation package.

8.6 Ideas for Action: Advanced Practices

Young leadership council. A petro-chemical company with which we have worked established a "young leadership council" as a shadow board from the ranks of their junior high-potentials. This council serves has access to most of the same reports as the executive board, and makes recommendations ahead of the executive board's decisions. It thereby challenges decision routines, provides a fresh perspective, and empowers strategic thinking beyond the upper echelons.

Red teaming. A practice we have seen mostly in the military, intelligence, and security communities involves designing a "red team" for important projects and decisions. This team is tasked with identifying points of failure, stress-testing critical assumptions, and providing challenges to the direction taken by senior management. Implementing this at scale points to an avenue of unfreezing rigid logics, especially if external experts are involved.

Open ecosystems. As described below in our case on Microsoft's transformation, Satya Nadella shook up management decision-making by bringing founder-CEOs of acquired start-ups to senior leadership offsites, even if their formal position in the reporting line wouldn't justify these invitations. This shows the potential for external partners to transform organizations—if they are positioned in powerful coalitions that can challenge established political stand-offs.

8.7 Collaborative Transformation in Action: Microsoft

> As to the methods, there may be a million and then some, but principles are few. The man who grasps the principles can successfully select his own methods. The man who tries methods, ignores principles, is sure to have trouble.—Ralph Waldo Emerson

In closing, let us consider the collaborative advantage behind one of the most spectacular transformations of our time. While each transformation is unique, and the particular recipes can never be perfectly replicated, we found in our research that there are still shared rhythms between success stories. Indeed, you will see that many of our lessons for using collaboration signatures to manage transformations echo in Satya Nadella's story.

As Nadella told us at a conference in Switzerland, when he took over as CEO of Microsoft in 2014, the company had a wildly one-sided emphasis on efficiency and legacy products. The single-minded focus on increasing efficiency was apparent, for example, in the stack-ranking performance management system. In this system, performance evaluations followed a fixed distribution, which meant that 10 percent of employees would always receive a poor rating, independent of their absolute level of contribution. This had helped create a cut-throat culture in which people were bent on identifying and eliminating mistakes—mostly the mistakes of others. In the words of a product manager: "If you don't play the politics, it's management by character assassination." The focus on protecting internal fiefdoms and monopolies was also apparent in Microsoft's aggressive opposition to open-source innovation, with then-chief executive Steve Ballmer calling Linux a cancer that attaches itself, in the sense of intellectual property, to everything it touches. Internal projects that were more innovative and boundary-spanning had a hard time: Potential market-busting businesses, such as e-book and smart phone technology, were killed or delayed amid bickering and power plays.

After a decade or so, the impact of this culture started to show: The market developed from desktop computers toward smartphones, from Microsoft's Windows to Apple's iPhone and Google's Android. The legacy part of the business was still going strong, with revenues tripling and profits doubling during Ballmer's tenure between 2000 and 2014, but the missing innovation and lack of transformation for the new age put into question the future viability of the company. The stock price was flat over that same period, even as the valuations of competitors, such as Apple and Google, soared to record highs. This affected employee moral: Ballmer's Glassdoor approval rating from his own employees was at a mere 29 percent. By comparison, Google CEO Larry Page commanded an approval rating of 94 percent, and that was even behind Facebook's Mark Zuckerberg, with 99 percent.

In diagnosing the problem, Nadella focused on an overreliance on hierarchies and structures, and too few autonomous, creative, and energized networks. Too little collaborative advantage, in other words: "Accountability—delivering on time and hitting numbers—trumped everything. Meetings were formal. If a senior leader wanted to tap the energy and creativity of someone lower down in the organization, she or he needed to invite that person's boss, and so on. Hierarchy and pecking order had taken control, and spontaneity and creativity had suffered." In order to transform Microsoft for a mobile- and cloud-first world, Nadella asked Kathleen Hogan to lead the cultural transformation as Chief People Officer.

Together, the two created an instant organization of champions, called the culture cabinet, to steer the transformation. Nadella and this team used a variety of relational levers to energize and guide the transformation: In order to change the relational dynamics within teams, Nadella assigned the book *Nonviolent Communication* to his leadership team. He increased cohesion of this team by encouraging them to "lean into each other's problems, promote dialogue, and be effective." In order to counteract groupthink, he promoted constructive disagreements in the leadership team: "Debate and argument are essential. Improving upon each other's ideas is crucial. I wanted people to speak up. 'Oh, here's a customer segmentation study I've done' 'Here's a pricing approach that contradicts that idea'. It's great to have good old-fashioned college debate. But there also has to be high-level agreement." At the same time, he focused intensely on increasing resonance and cohesion: "They were all very talented people, but the senior leadership team needed to become a cohesive team that shared a common world view... We needed everyone to view the senior leadership team as his or her first team, not just another meeting they attended. We needed to be aligned on mission, strategy and culture."

You might be reminded here of the crucial role of the economic development board in the case of Singapore, or the forums in the case of IBM...

Nadella also used collaborative advantage to break up echo chambers and bringing in new perspectives. For example, he brought the CEOs of innovative companies Microsoft had acquired into the senior leadership network, even though they didn't formally qualify: "These new Microsoft leaders were mission-oriented, innovative, born in the mobile-first and cloud-first world," says Nadella "I knew we could learn from their fresh, outside perspective. The only problem was that most of these leaders didn't officially 'qualify' to go to executive retreats given the person's level in the organization. To make matters worse, neither did their manager, or even their manager's manager... Inviting them was not one of my more popular decisions. But they showed up bright-eyed, completely ignorant of the history they were breaking. They asked questions. They shared their own journeys. They pushed us to be better."

Similar Döpfner at Springer, he created powerful new coalitions to shake up the collaboration signature at Microsoft and advocate for the digital-first mindset.

In order to increase trust and safety, Nadella focused on transforming mindsets into Growth Mindsets. In his own words, he was aiming to transform Microsoft employees from Know-it-alls to Learn-it-alls. Instead of a cut-throat culture of internal competition, leaders should nurture an environment based on "the belief that everyone can grow and develop; potential is nurtured, not pre-determined; and anyone can change their mindset." In order to achieve this change, Microsoft also worked with social psychologists from Raphael's old scientific home at Stanford University. This was further reinforced with formal processes. For example, internal focus groups were established to enable bottom-up inputs to enter into the transformation.

All of this lay a foundation for change, and improved Microsoft's capacity to absorb new ideas and adapt to relational impetus from the new coalitions in the network.

The network of transformation agents embarked on many initiatives to transform the culture: "We never believed there would be one thing that could change the company. It would be a lot of things, big and small, reinforcing the change. Some were more systemic and process oriented, such as getting rid of the performance stack evaluation system. Some were symbolic, such as distributing napkins with the symbol for 'listen' printed on them in the cafeteria. And some were strongly focused on relational incentives. Nudges, practices, process changes and symbols were employed to reinforce the transformation."

For example, the leadership team focused on creating "immersive experiences" for leaders to engage intensely with customers on their own turf. "Getting to know each other in the context of solving a partner's problem was more meaningful than rope exercises or off-site discussions," explained the transformation champion behind this proposal. Consider how these relational incentives resemble the obligatory study trips for board members in the case of VM's transformation.

Other, more typical examples include the Hackathon, which creates a relational format for employees from nominally different tribes to come together and innovate jointly. Leadership behavior also had to be transformed. For example, leaders were asked to close meetings with a quick reflection, whether this was a growth-mindset or a fixed-mindset meeting.

After four years of hard and diligent work nurturing the collaborative advantage at Microsoft, the results have begun to show. Employee morale is up, and Nadella's approval rating stands at 95 percent. Microsoft is rated as one of the five best AI companies to work for. The combination of existing capabilities and new, explorative working in the cloud world have resulted in over 95 percent of Fortune 500 companies using Azure, Microsoft's cloud service. Finally, the stock market believes in Microsoft's potential again: the transformation helped market cap top *$1 trillion* for the first time in June 2019. (As of this book's publication, it hovers over $2 trillion). This represents an *eightfold increase in value* in the years of Nadella's tenure. Microsoft's continued role in pushing the boundaries of generative AI with the ChatGPT platform and their partnership with OpenAI further underscores the impressive transformation Nadella has led.

> **Lesson Learned:**
> What can we learn from Microsofts's collaborative transformation?
> Through many small and big initiatives, reaching from systemic and process-oriented changes to relational incentives to symbolic nudges, it is possible to successfully reinforce change and transform a company, characterized by hierarchies and formal structures, into a collaborative and energizing workplace.
> How? It is all about building collaborative advantage:
>
> - Counteract groupthink and promote dialogue, constructive disagreements, and joint problem-solving in the leadership team
> - Increase resonance and cohesion through an aligned mission, strategy, and culture
> - Break up echo chambers and bring in new, outside perspectives
> - Bring together employees from nominally different tribes so they can innovate together
> - Build up a growth mindset among employees: from Know-it-alls to Learn-it-alls
> - Close meetings with a quick reflection, whether this was a growth-mindset or a fixed-mindset meeting
> - Establish internal focus groups to enable bottom-up inputs into the transformation
> - Bring in powerful new coalitions to foster the collaboration signature
> - Focus on engagement with your customers

8.8 The Next Step

If you want to turbocharge collaborative transformation for your organization, go to collaborative-advantage.org/transformation for suggestions and resources on how to get started. Among other items, you will find:

- A one-hour sample workshop discussing the potential of collaborative transformation and potential action items with your relevant stakeholders (complete with agenda, pre-reads, suggested slides, and outcomes)
- A video of a senior leader's personal reflections on collaborative transformation

You can also scan the QR Code if you don't like typing. The resources are all free.

> Thank you for reading. We hope it was helpful. If you have any questions, you can reach us at:
>
> - Raphael: https://www.linkedin.com/in/raphael-boemelburg/
> - Oliver: https://www.linkedin.com/in/olivergassmann/
> - More resources: https://www.collaborative-advantage.org/
>
> You can also always reach us via email: Raphael.boemelburg@unisg.ch
> If you feel inclined to help *us* out, the best way to do that is by posting a review on Amazon, sending us feedback and suggestions, or recommending this book to a friend or colleague.
> We wish you the very best—and count on leaders such as you to deliver the future.

Reference

In order to keep the book lean enough to comfortably be read on a plane, we have listed the full references on the companion website for your convenience. If you want to dig deeper, please check them out here:

11. Collaborative-advantage.org/references-transformation/11.

Index

A
adaptability 7, 40, 56, 99, 115, 136, 166
agility 5, 15, 20, 172, 173
AI in business 3
Amazon 9, 124–129, 196
Apple 6, 7, 58, 123, 141, 191

B
Bridgewater Associates 36, 106

C
change 4, 5, 7, 9, 12, 13, 15, 18, 23, 24, 29–36, 38, 40, 43, 53, 54, 56, 62, 64, 68, 69, 77, 82, 85, 86, 98, 99, 106, 118, 119, 121, 126, 135, 141, 142, 146, 148–150, 153–163, 165–167, 170, 172, 175, 176, 184, 185, 189, 190, 192–195

collaboration 7, 9–15, 19, 20, 22, 23, 32–35, 38, 40, 41, 43, 44, 47, 48, 50–59, 64, 65, 67, 69, 70, 80–100, 102–111, 116, 117, 121–125, 127, 129, 141, 143–146, 148, 152–155, 158–160, 165, 170–174, 180–184, 186, 188, 191, 193, 195
collaborative advantage 7, 9, 10, 23, 24, 44, 53, 60, 64, 65, 68–70, 81, 82, 91, 93, 96–99, 104, 106, 107, 109, 111, 116, 118, 122, 123, 127, 129, 143, 144, 146–156, 160, 161, 163, 166, 169, 174, 179, 180, 184, 191–195
Corporate Entrepreneurship 29–45, 47–71, 75–100, 135–177
Covestro 161–164, 189, 190
culture 10, 12, 14, 21–23, 31, 32, 41, 48, 56, 57, 60, 69, 87, 118, 119, 121, 124, 126, 135,

136, 147, 162, 164–166, 168–172, 175, 176, 181, 186, 187, 190–195
customer innovation 8, 12, 32, 33, 69, 162

D

Daimler 7, 58, 170–174, 187, 189
data 11, 12, 14, 15, 21–23, 33, 41, 83–85, 89, 106, 123–125, 127, 139, 141, 149
data-driven management 21, 23
digitalization 162, 175, 176, 185
Disney 141, 182, 183
disruption 3, 31, 114, 168
Dyson 50, 51, 123

E

ecosystems 5, 7–9, 18, 49, 75, 80, 87–91, 121

G

growth 4, 9, 21, 31, 41, 54, 76–80, 82, 83, 86, 87, 118, 119, 121, 127, 141, 168, 179, 186, 194, 195

H

Hilti v, 29–33, 38
hyper-growth 8, 80, 82, 90, 91, 124, 129

I

innovation 3, 8–10, 12–15, 17, 30, 32, 33, 35, 36, 40–42, 44, 47–50, 52, 53, 55–59, 64, 66–70, 80, 99, 103, 123, 126, 127, 129, 137, 140, 162–165, 170, 172, 174, 180, 192
intrapreneurship 171

L

leadership 9, 10, 13, 21, 41, 59, 77, 78, 82, 89, 112–114, 116, 119, 123, 141, 142, 145, 146, 148, 149, 152–154, 165, 169, 181, 183, 187, 189, 191–195
learning 33–35, 37, 40, 41, 50, 55, 62, 65, 78, 79, 97, 98, 112, 113, 117, 121, 122, 145, 148, 149, 151, 166, 190
Lego 68–70, 123

M

Microsoft v, 7, 10, 59, 60, 140, 191–194

N

networks 7–9, 23, 35, 37, 41, 42, 44, 55, 57, 64, 66, 80, 81, 83, 89, 90, 104, 127–129, 137, 140, 141, 144, 163–166, 168, 169, 172–174, 186, 189, 192, 194

O

open innovation 69
organizational design 119, 121
Otto v, 175, 176

P

people analytics 24
Pixar 116, 179–184, 190

R

renewal 6, 29, 32, 140, 141, 169, 174
Rocket Internet 75–80, 82

S

Samsung 67, 135–143
scale-ups 79, 95
Scaling 77, 80, 81, 86, 87, 90, 91, 99, 104, 106, 118, 121, 122, 124, 125, 129, 130, 166
smart enterprise 23
speed 3, 6, 7, 11, 45, 61, 63, 76–79, 84, 88, 94, 115, 116, 128, 166, 173, 185, 188
Springer v, 141, 184–188, 190, 193
start-up cooperation 69, 137

T

transformation 7, 9, 12, 14, 15, 21, 23, 29, 31, 52, 54, 56, 83, 98, 99, 118, 119, 128, 141, 143, 144, 146–150, 152–156, 158, 161–166, 168–170, 173–177, 184, 185, 187–195

U

unicorns 75, 176

V

Valve 59–64, 68, 123
VUCA 5, 7, 8
volatility 35, 115

GPSR Compliance

The European Union's (EU) General Product Safety Regulation (GPSR) is a set of rules that requires consumer products to be safe and our obligations to ensure this.

If you have any concerns about our products, you can contact us on

ProductSafety@springernature.com

In case Publisher is established outside the EU, the EU authorized representative is:

Springer Nature Customer Service Center GmbH
Europaplatz 3
69115 Heidelberg, Germany

www.ingramcontent.com/pod-product-compliance
Lightning Source LLC
LaVergne TN
LVHW050013270326
834688LV00069B/131